The History of Ancient Israel

Completely Synchronizing the Extra-Biblical Apocrypha Books of Enoch, Jasher, and Jubilees

Book Six

From Goshen to Sinai

Ahava Lilburn

Minister **2** Others

The History of Ancient Israel series
was first published under the title
Ancient Texts and the Bible.
This is the updated and repackaged version of the first set.

Copyright © 2021 Ahava Lilburn/Minister 2 Others
All rights reserved.

Minister2others.com

Cover and chapter images by
Katia Petrunina
Used with permission.

www.behance.net/babayuka

Ancient manuscripts compiled for this series:

The Bible
King James Version 1769

The Book of Enoch
An English translation by Dr. Laurence,
Archbishop of Cashel,
Formerly professor of Hebrew at Oxford, 1833

The Book of Jasher
Faithfully translated 1840
From the original Hebrew into English
Published by J.H. Parry & Company 1887

The Book of Jubilees
By R.H. Charles, Oxford: Clarendon Press, 1913

The History of Ancient Israel

Completely Synchronizing the Extra-Biblical Apocrypha Books of Enoch, Jasher, and Jubilees

Book 1:   From Adam to Noah
Book 2:   From Noah to Abraham
Book 3:   From Abraham to Israel
Book 4:   From Israel to Egypt
Book 5:   From Egypt to Goshen
Book 6:   From Goshen to Sinai
Book 7:   From Sinai to the Tabernacle
Book 8:   Through the Book of Leviticus
Book 9:   Through the Book of Numbers
Book 10: Through the Book of Joshua

Contents

Introduction

Exodus: Chapter One	1
Exodus: Chapter Two	41
Exodus: Chapter Three	101
Exodus: Chapter Four	107
Exodus: Chapter Five	115
Exodus: Chapter Six	121
Exodus: Chapter Seven	127
Exodus: Chapter Eight	137
Exodus: Chapter Nine	145
Exodus: Chapter Ten	153
Exodus: Chapter Eleven	159
Exodus: Chapter Twelve	161
Exodus: Chapter Thirteen	177
Exodus: Chapter Fourteen	183
Exodus: Chapter Fifteen	195
Exodus: Chapter Sixteen	201
Exodus: Chapter Seventeen	209
Exodus: Chapter Eighteen	213
Exodus: Chapter Nineteen	219
Exodus: Chapter Twenty	223

Introduction

By now, you have more than likely read the first five books of THE HISTORY OF ANCIENT ISRAEL series, which means you're halfway through the series! You've gone through the book of Genesis and are ready to explore the next phase. I hope you have found this journey delightful and interesting! You have journeyed from the time of Creation to Joseph's death. Now, get your drink and settle into your favorite reading spot as you prepare to enter into the book of Exodus, the sixth book of the series! You can now explore more details concerning Joseph's death and travel to the time of Moses and the Ten Commandments. Remember, in this series, the extra-Biblical texts of Enoch, Jasher, and Jubilees have been interwoven through the verses of the Bible in their proper chronological order, so you are able to study through without worrying about figuring out their order on your own. The Torah was used with great care to ensure all information was entered in the proper order for the entire series of THE HISTORY OF ANCIENT ISRAEL.

By reading through THE HISTORY OF ANCIENT ISRAEL series, you will examine the historical events found throughout the pages of the Bible. You will be amazed at what comes into play once the Books of Enoch, Jasher, and Jubilees are taken into account.

You might wonder why you would want the added details concerning these stories since you already know them so well. By reading through these stories, a new understanding begins to take place as you fill in the once overlooked voids. Since this information is being woven together through THE HISTORY OF ANCIENT ISRAEL series, it is easy to read the stories and gather these extra little (sometimes very significant) details that might help bring clarity to some of the situations. By seeing a whole new side to the stories, you can relate to the characters in a more profound way than you had before. For instance, what happens in Egypt after all the sons of Jacob and the brethren of Joseph were dead; how did the Egyptians react and why? Read through THE HISTORY OF ANCIENT ISRAEL series and find out.

Each additional scene from the Books of Enoch, Jasher, and Jubilees will show different sides of the people and their lives, which, in turn, will help to make this history feel new again. These details can help you better understand why certain decisions were made or why some things transpired the way they did. The additional information will keep you on your toes as you study through the series, which was not assembled to replace or "add to" what is already written in the Bible, but rather to show the consistencies throughout the books. These are simply extra-Biblical texts with added details to the stories you already know. THE HISTORY OF ANCIENT ISRAEL series is assembled into proper chronological order to make it easier to read and study them. These books can be used as a read-aloud text for you and others, as a study guide for a book group, or read for the sheer pleasure of reading.

There are so many extra details of what happens in Egypt after Joseph and those who remembered him are gone, you will be amazed at the various information there is to read through, and it will leave you wanting to know more and more. Do you know about Zepho and his reign? What happened in the battles between the Egyptians and the children of Israel? What happens to the children of Israel after these battles? How did the Israelites move on? How did they handle the events that occurred and still stand by God?

You already know the Pharaoh called for all male children to be killed; through these documents, you will discover even more concerning the hows and whys this happened. Explore the various ways that the children of Israel found to keep their children alive. Read more about Moses' birth and his first few months and years. Did you know that there once was a time when Moses reigned over Cush? Do you know how old he was when he started his reign? Or how long he stood in this position of authority? What happened to end his reign? Did you know he served prison time in the dungeon of Reuel's house? Examine these stories and so much more in this book from THE HISTORY OF ANCIENT ISRAEL series. It is filled with so many extra details that you will want to share it with your family and friends!

Did you know there were lions guarding the house of Pharaoh when Moses and Aaron arrived to talk to Pharaoh? What events transpired when Moses set the lions free? And what new information is written in these manuscripts concerning the plagues that came upon Egypt? Greater detail about this time period abounds in this book!

Look at all that happened pertaining to the night the firstborn of all the land was wiped out. See the reactions when the Egyptians awoke to so much death. This monumental event was the final straw for the Pharaoh, and he finally set the children of Israel free. Once liberated, Moses leads the Children of Israel out of Egypt and on towards the Promised Land. This journey is not as easy going as one would suspect, however. What other exciting twists and turns are brought to light through these little known manuscripts?

The books in THE HISTORY OF ANCIENT ISRAEL series are woven together in such a way that it is easy to read and study. The extra text is clearly labeled, so you know what has been inserted and where. THE HISTORY OF ANCIENT ISRAEL series is formatted and printed in the same fashion as the Bible, with the exception of the additional verses from the books of Enoch, Jasher, and Jubilees. Although the words "thou" and "thine" have been replaced with words like "you" and "your" for easier reading, the integrity of each verse remains intact. Enjoy studying through these books on your own or with your Bible Study group and discover for yourself all that the extra-biblical texts have to show us!

Exodus: Chapter One

(Exodus 1:1)
>Now these are the names of the children of Israel, which came into Egypt; every man and his household came with Jacob.

(Exodus 1:2)
>Reuben, Simeon, Levi, and Judah,

(Exodus 1:3)
>Issachar, Zebulun, and Benjamin,

(Exodus 1:4)
>Dan, and Naphtali, Gad, and Asher.

(Exodus 1:5)
>And all the souls that came out of the loins of Jacob were seventy souls: for Joseph was in Egypt already.

(Exodus 1:6)
>And Joseph died, and all his brethren, and all that generation.

>(Jasher 63:1)
>And in the ninety-third year Levi died, the son of Jacob, in Egypt, and Levi was a hundred and thirty-seven years old when he died, and they put him into a coffin and he was given into the hands of his children.

(Jasher 63:2)
And it came to pass after the death of Levi, when all Egypt saw that the sons of Jacob the brethren of Joseph were dead, all the Egyptians began to afflict the children of Jacob, and to embitter their lives from that day to the day of their going forth from Egypt, and they took from their hands all the vineyards and fields which Joseph had given to them, and all the elegant houses in which the people of Israel lived, and all the fat of Egypt, the Egyptians took all from the sons of Jacob in those days.

(Exodus 1:7)
And the children of Israel were fruitful, and increased abundantly, and multiplied, and waxed exceeding mighty; and the land was filled with them.

(Jasher 63:3)
And the hand of all Egypt became more grievous in those days against the children of Israel, and the Egyptians injured the Israelites until the children of Israel were wearied of their lives on account of the Egyptians.

(Exodus 1:8) (Jasher 63:4)
And it came to pass in those days, in the hundred and second year of Israel's going down to Egypt, that Pharaoh king of Egypt died. Now there arose up a new king, Melol his son, who reigned in his stead over Egypt. And all the mighty men of Egypt and all that generation which knew not Joseph and his brethren died in those days.

(Jasher 63:5)
And another generation rose up in their stead, which had not known the sons of Jacob and all the good which they had done to them, and all their might in Egypt.

Book Six: From Goshen to Sinai

(Jasher 63:6)
Therefore all Egypt began from that day forth to embitter the lives of the sons of Jacob, and to afflict them with all manner of hard labor, because they had not known their ancestors who had delivered them in the days of the famine.

(Jasher 63:7)
And this was also from the Lord, for the children of Israel, to benefit them in their latter days, in order that all the children of Israel might know the Lord their God.

(Jasher 63:8)
And in order to know the signs and mighty wonders which the Lord would do in Egypt on account of his people Israel, in order that the children of Israel might fear the Lord God of their ancestors, and walk in all his ways, they and their seed after them all the days.

(Jasher 63:9)
Melol was twenty years old when he began to reign, and he reigned ninety-four years, and all Egypt called his name Pharaoh after the name of his father, as it was their custom to do to every king who reigned over them in Egypt.

(Jasher 63:10)
At that time all the troops of Angeas king of Africa went forth to spread along the land of Chittim as usual for plunder.

(Jasher 63:11)
And Zepho the son of Eliphaz the son of Esau heard their report, and he went forth to meet them with his army, and he fought them there in the road.

(Jasher 63:12)
And Zepho smote the troops of the king of Africa with the edge of the sword, and left none remaining of them, and not even one returned to his master in Africa.

(Jasher 63:13)
And Angeas heard of this which Zepho the son of Eliphaz had done to all his troops, that he had destroyed them, and Angeas assembled all his troops, all the men of the land of Africa, a people numerous like the sand by the sea shore.

(Jasher 63:14)
And Angeas sent to Lucus his brother, saying, Come to me with all your men and help me to smite Zepho and all the children of Chittim who have destroyed my men, and Lucus came with his whole army, a very great force, to assist Angeas his brother to fight with Zepho and the children of Chittim.

(Jasher 63:15)
And Zepho and the children of Chittim heard this thing, and they were greatly afraid and a great terror fell upon their hearts.

(Jasher 63:16)
And Zepho also sent a letter to the land of Edom to Hadad the son of Bedad king of Edom and to all the children of Esau, saying,

(Jasher 63:17)
I have heard that Angeas king of Africa is coming to us with his brother for battle against us, and we are greatly afraid of him, for his army is very great, particularly as he comes against us with his brother and his army likewise.

(Jasher 63:18)
Now therefore come also up with me and help me, and we will fight together against Angeas and his brother Lucus, and you will save us out of their hands, but if not, know that we shall all die.

(Jasher 63:19)
And the children of Esau sent a letter to the children of Chittim and to Zepho their king, saying, We cannot fight against Angeas and his people for a covenant of peace has been between us these many years, from the days of Bela the first king, and from the days of Joseph the son of Jacob king of Egypt, with whom we fought on the other side of Jordan when he buried his father.

(Jasher 63:20)
And when Zepho heard the words of his brethren the children of Esau he refrained from them, and Zepho was greatly afraid of Angeas.

(Jasher 63:21)
And Angeas and Lucus his brother arrayed all their forces, about eight hundred thousand men, against the children of Chittim.

(Jasher 63:22)
And all the children of Chittim said to Zepho, Pray for us to the God of your ancestors, peradventure he may deliver us from the hand of Angeas and his army, for we have heard that he is a great God and that he delivers all who trust in him.

(Jasher 63:23)
And Zepho heard their words, and Zepho sought the Lord and he said,

(Jasher 63:24)
o Lord God of Abraham and Isaac my ancestors, this day I know that you are a true God, and all the gods of the nations are vain and useless.

(Jasher 63:25)
Remember now this day to me your covenant with Abraham our father, which our ancestors related to us, and do graciously with me this day for the sake of Abraham and Isaac our fathers, and save me and the children of Chittim from the hand of the king of Africa who comes against us for battle.

(Jasher 63:26)
And the Lord hearkened to the voice of Zepho, and he had regard for him on account of Abraham and Isaac, and the Lord delivered Zepho and the children of Chittim from the hand of Angeas and his people.

(Jasher 63:27)
And Zepho fought Angeas king of Africa and all his people on that day, and the Lord gave all the people of Angeas into the hands of the children of Chittim.

(Jasher 63:28)
And the battle was severe upon Angeas, and Zepho smote all the men of Angeas and Lucus his brother, with the edge of the sword, and there fell from them to the evening of that day about four hundred thousand men.

(Jasher 63:29)
And when Angeas saw that all his men perished, he sent a letter to all the inhabitants of Africa to come to him, to assist him in the battle, and he wrote in the letter, saying, All who are found in Africa let them come to me from ten years old

and upward; let them all come to me, and behold if he comes not he shall die, and all that he has, with his whole household, the king will take.

(Jasher 63:30)
And all the rest of the inhabitants of Africa were terrified at the words of Angeas, and there went out of the city about three hundred thousand men and boys, from ten years upward, and they came to Angeas.

(Jasher 63:31)
And at the end of ten days Angeas renewed the battle against Zepho and the children of Chittim, and the battle was very great and strong between them.

(Jasher 63:32)
And from the army of Angeas and Lucus, Zepho sent many of the wounded to his hand, about two thousand men, and Sosiphtar the captain of the host of Angeas fell in that battle.

(Jasher 63:33)
And when Sosiphtar had fallen, the African troops turned their backs to flee, and they fled, and Angeas and Lucus his brother were with them.

(Jasher 63:34)
And Zepho and the children of Chittim pursued them, and they smote them still heavily on the road, about two hundred men, and they pursued Azdrubal the son of Angeas who had fled with his father, and they smote twenty of his men in the road, and Azdrubal escaped from the children of Chittim, and they did not slay him.

(Jasher 63:35)
And Angeas and Lucus his brother fled with the rest of their men, and they escaped and came into Africa with terror and consternation, and Angeas feared all the days lest Zepho the son of Eliphaz should go to war with him.

~ ~ ~

(Jasher 64:1)
And Balaam the son of Beor was at that time with Angeas in the battle, and when he saw that Zepho prevailed over Angeas, he fled from there and came to Chittim.

(Jasher 64:2)
And Zepho and the children of Chittim received him with great honor, for Zepho knew Balaam's wisdom, and Zepho gave to Balaam many gifts and he remained with him.

(Jasher 64:3)
And when Zepho had returned from the war, he commanded all the children of Chittim to be numbered who had gone into battle with him, and behold not one was missed.

(Jasher 64:4)
And Zepho rejoiced at this thing, and he renewed his kingdom, and he made a feast to all his subjects.

(Jasher 64:5)
But Zepho remembered not the Lord and considered not that the Lord had helped him in battle, and that he had delivered him and his people from the hand of the king of Africa, but still walked in the ways of the children of Chittim and the wicked

children of Esau, to serve other gods which his brothers the children of Esau had taught him; it is therefore said, From the wicked goes forth wickedness.

(Jasher 64:6)
And Zepho reigned over all the children of Chittim securely, but knew not the Lord who had delivered him and all his people from the hand of the king of Africa; and the troops of Africa came no more to Chittim to plunder as usual, for they knew of the power of Zepho who had smitten them all at the edge of the sword, so Angeas was afraid of Zepho the son of Eliphaz, and of the children of Chittim all the days.

(Jasher 64:7)
At that time when Zepho had returned from the war, and when Zepho had seen how he prevailed over all the people of Africa and had smitten them in battle at the edge of the sword, then Zepho advised with the children of Chittim, to go to Egypt to fight with the sons of Jacob and with Pharaoh king of Egypt.

(Jasher 64:8)
For Zepho heard that the mighty men of Egypt were dead and that Joseph and his brethren the sons at Jacob were dead, and that all their children the children of Israel remained in Egypt.

(Jasher 64:9)
And Zepho considered to go to fight against them and all Egypt, to avenge the cause of his brethren the children of Esau, whom Joseph with his brethren and all Egypt had smitten in the land of Canaan, when they went up to bury Jacob in Hebron.

(Jasher 64:10)
And Zepho sent messengers to Hadad, son of Bedad, king of Edom, and to all his brethren the children of Esau, saying,

(Jasher 64:11)
Did you not say that you would not fight against the king of Africa for he is a member of your covenant? Behold I fought with him and smote him and all his people.

(Jasher 64:12)
Now therefore I have resolved to fight against Egypt and the children of Jacob who are there, and I will be revenged of them for what Joseph, his brothers and ancestors did to us in the land of Canaan when they went up to bury their father in Hebron.

(Jasher 64:13)
Now then if you are willing to come to me to assist me in fighting against them and Egypt, then shall we avenge the cause of our brothers.

(Jasher 64:14)
And the children of Esau hearkened to the words of Zepho, and the children of Esau gathered themselves together, a very great people, and they went to assist Zepho and the children of Chittim in battle.

(Jasher 64:15)
And Zepho sent to all the children of the east and to all the children of Ishmael with words like to these, and they gathered themselves and came to the assistance of Zepho and the children of Chittim in the war upon Egypt.

Book Six: From Goshen to Sinai

(Jasher 64:16)
And all these kings, the king of Edom and the children of the east, and all the children of Ishmael, and Zepho the king of Chittim went forth and arrayed all their hosts in Hebron.

(Jasher 64:17)
And the camp was very heavy, extending in length a distance of three days' journey, a people numerous as the sand upon the sea shore which can not be counted.

(Jasher 64:18)
And all these kings and their hosts went down and came against all Egypt in battle, and encamped together in the valley of Pathros.

(Jasher 64:19)
And all Egypt heard their report, and they also gathered themselves together, all the people of the land of Egypt, and of all the cities belonging to Egypt, about three hundred thousand men.

(Jubilees 46:9...)
And the king of Egypt went forth to war with the king of Canaan in the forty-seventh jubilee, in the second week in the second year.

(Jasher 64:20)
And the men of Egypt sent also to the children of Israel who were in those days in the land of Goshen, to come to them in order to go and fight with these kings.

(...Jubilees 46:9)
And the children of Israel brought forth all the bones of the children of Jacob save the bones of Joseph, and they buried

them in the field in the double cave in the mountain.

(Jasher 64:21)
And the men of Israel assembled and were about one hundred and fifty men, and they went into battle to assist the Egyptians.

(Jasher 64:22)
And the men of Israel and of Egypt went forth, about three hundred thousand men and one hundred and fifty men, and they went toward these kings to battle, and they placed themselves from without the land of Goshen opposite Pathros.

(Jasher 64:23)
And the Egyptians believed not in Israel to go with them in their camps together for battle, for all the Egyptians said, Perhaps the children of Israel will deliver us into the hand of the children of Esau and Ishmael, for they are their brethren.

(Jasher 64:24)
And all the Egyptians said to the children of Israel, Remain here together in your stand and we will go and fight against the children of Esau and Ishmael, and if these kings should prevail over us, then come altogether upon them and assist us, and the children of Israel did so.

(Jasher 64:25)
And Zepho the son of Eliphaz the son of Esau king of Chittim, and Hadad the son of Bedad king of Edom, and all their camps, and all the children of the east, and children of Ishmael, a people numerous as sand, encamped together in the valley of Pathros opposite Tachpanches.

(Jasher 64:26)
And Balaam the son of Beor the Syrian was there in the camp

of Zepho, for he came with the children of Chittim to the battle, and Balaam was a man highly honored in the eyes of Zepho and his men.

(Jasher 64:27)
And Zepho said to Balaam, Try by divination for us that we may know who will prevail in the battle, we or the Egyptians.

(Jasher 64:28)
And Balaam rose up and tried the are of divination, and he was skillful in the knowledge of it, but he was confused and the work was destroyed in his hand.

(Jasher 64:29)
And he tried it again but it did not succeed, and Balaam despaired of it and left it and did not complete it, for this was from the Lord, in order to cause Zepho and his people to fall into the hand of the children of Israel, who had trusted in the Lord, the God of their ancestors, in their war.

(Jasher 64:30)
And Zepho and Hadad put their forces in battle array, and all the Egyptians went alone against them, about three hundred thousand men, and not one man of Israel was with them.

(Jasher 64:31)
And all the Egyptians fought with these kings opposite Pathros and Tachpanches, and the battle was severe against the Egyptians.

(Jasher 64:32)
And the kings were stronger than the Egyptians in that battle, and about one hundred and eighty men of Egypt fell on that day, and about thirty men of the forces of the kings, and all

the men of Egypt fled from before the kings, so the children of Esau and Ishmael pursued the Egyptians, continuing to smite them to the place where was the camp of the children of Israel.

(Jasher 64:33)
And all the Egyptians cried to the children of Israel, saying, Hasten to us and assist us and save us from the hand of Esau, Ishmael and the children of Chittim.

(Jasher 64:34)
And the hundred and fifty men of the children of Israel ran from their station to the camps of these kings, and the children of Israel cried to the Lord their God to deliver them.

(Jasher 64:35)
And the Lord hearkened to Israel, and the Lord gave all the men of the kings into their hand, and the children of Israel fought against these kings, and the children of Israel smote about four thousand of the kings' men.

(Jasher 64:36)
And the Lord threw a great consternation in the camp of the kings, so that the fear of the children of Israel fell upon them.

(Jasher 64:37)
And all the hosts of the kings fled from before the children of Israel and the children of Israel pursued them continuing to smite them to the borders of the land of Cush.

(Jasher 64:38)
And the children of Israel slew of them in the road yet two thousand men, and of the children of Israel not one fell.

(Jasher 64:39)
And when the Egyptians saw that the children of Israel had fought with such few men with the kings, and that the battle was so very severe against them,

(Jasher 64:40)
All the Egyptians were greatly afraid of their lives on account of the strong battle, and all Egypt fled, every man hiding himself from the arrayed forces, and they hid themselves in the road, and they left the Israelites to fight.

(Jasher 64:41)
And the children of Israel inflicted a terrible blow upon the kings' men, and they returned from them after they had driven them to the border of the land of Cush.

(Jasher 64:42)
And all Israel knew the thing which the men of Egypt had done to them, that they had fled from them in battle, and had left them to fight alone.

(Jasher 64:43)
So the children of Israel also acted with cunning, and as the children of Israel returned from battle, they found some of the Egyptians in the road and smote them there.

(Jasher 64:44)
And while they slew them, they said to them these words:

(Jasher 64:45)
Wherefore did you go from us and leave us, being a few people, to fight against these kings who had a great people to smite us, that you might thereby deliver your own souls?

(Jasher 64:46)
And of some which the Israelites met on the road, they the children of Israel spoke to each other, saying, Smite, smite, for he is an Ishmaelite, or an Edomite, or from the children of Chittim, and they stood over him and slew him, and they knew that he was an Egyptian.

(Jasher 64:47)
And the children of Israel did these things cunningly against the Egyptians, because they had deserted them in battle and had fled from them.

(Jasher 64:48)
And the children of Israel slew of the men of Egypt in the road in this manner, about two hundred men.

(Jasher 64:49)
And all the men of Egypt saw the evil which the children of Israel had done to them, so all Egypt feared greatly the children of Israel, for they had seen their great power, and that not one man of them had fallen.

(Jasher 64:50)
So all the children of Israel returned with joy on their road to Goshen, and the rest of Egypt returned each man to his place.

(Jubilees 46:10)
And the most of them returned to Egypt, but a few of them remained in the mountains of Hebron, and Amram your father remained with them.

(Jubilees 46:11)
And the king of Canaan was victorious over the king of Egypt, and he closed the gates of Egypt.

Book Six: From Goshen to Sinai

~ ~ ~

(Jasher 65:1)
And it came to pass after these things, that all the counselors of Pharaoh, king of Egypt, and all the elders of Egypt assembled and came before the king and bowed down to the ground, and they sat before him.

(Jasher 65:2)
And the counselors and elders of Egypt spoke to the king, saying,

(Jasher 65:3)
Behold the people of the children of Israel is greater and mightier than we are, and you know all the evil which they did to us in the road when we returned from battle.

(Jasher 65:4)
And you have also seen their strong power, for this power is to them from their fathers, for but a few men stood up against a people numerous as the sand, and smote them at the edge of the sword, and of themselves not one has fallen, so that if they had been numerous they would then have utterly destroyed them.

(Jasher 65:5)
Now therefore give us counsel what to do with them, until we gradually destroy them from among us, lest they become too numerous for us in the land.

(Jasher 65:6)
For if the children of Israel should increase in the land, they will become an obstacle to us, and if any war should happen to

take place, they with their great strength will join our enemy against us, and fight against us, destroy us from the land and go away from it.

(Exodus 1:9) (Jasher 65:7...) (Jubilees 46:12)
So the king devised an evil device against the children of Israel of afflicting them and answered the elders of Egypt and he said to his people, Behold, the people of the children of Israel have increased and multiplied more than we, and they are more and mightier than we are.

(Exodus 1:10) (Jubilees 46:13)
Come on, let us deal wisely with them; lest they multiply, and become too many and let us afflict them with slavery before it come to pass, that, when there falls out any war, they join also to our enemies, and fight against us, and so get them up out of the land for their hearts and faces are towards the land of Canaan.

(...Jasher 65:7)
This is the plan advised against Israel, from which we will not depart,

(Jasher 65:8)
Behold in the land are Pithom and Rameses, cities unfortified against battle, it behooves you and us to build them, and to fortify them.

(Jasher 65:9)
Now therefore go you also and act cunningly toward them, and proclaim a voice in Egypt and in Goshen at the command of the king, saying,

Book Six: From Goshen to Sinai

~ ~ ~

(Jasher 65:1)
And it came to pass after these things, that all the counselors of Pharaoh, king of Egypt, and all the elders of Egypt assembled and came before the king and bowed down to the ground, and they sat before him.

(Jasher 65:2)
And the counselors and elders of Egypt spoke to the king, saying,

(Jasher 65:3)
Behold the people of the children of Israel is greater and mightier than we are, and you know all the evil which they did to us in the road when we returned from battle.

(Jasher 65:4)
And you have also seen their strong power, for this power is to them from their fathers, for but a few men stood up against a people numerous as the sand, and smote them at the edge of the sword, and of themselves not one has fallen, so that if they had been numerous they would then have utterly destroyed them.

(Jasher 65:5)
Now therefore give us counsel what to do with them, until we gradually destroy them from among us, lest they become too numerous for us in the land.

(Jasher 65:6)
For if the children of Israel should increase in the land, they will become an obstacle to us, and if any war should happen to

take place, they with their great strength will join our enemy against us, and fight against us, destroy us from the land and go away from it.

(Exodus 1:9) (Jasher 65:7...) (Jubilees 46:12)
So the king devised an evil device against the children of Israel of afflicting them and answered the elders of Egypt and he said to his people, Behold, the people of the children of Israel have increased and multiplied more than we, and they are more and mightier than we are.

(Exodus 1:10) (Jubilees 46:13)
Come on, let us deal wisely with them; lest they multiply, and become too many and let us afflict them with slavery before it come to pass, that, when there falls out any war, they join also to our enemies, and fight against us, and so get them up out of the land for their hearts and faces are towards the land of Canaan.

(...Jasher 65:7)
This is the plan advised against Israel, from which we will not depart,

(Jasher 65:8)
Behold in the land are Pithom and Rameses, cities unfortified against battle, it behooves you and us to build them, and to fortify them.

(Jasher 65:9)
Now therefore go you also and act cunningly toward them, and proclaim a voice in Egypt and in Goshen at the command of the king, saying,

Book Six: From Goshen to Sinai

(Jasher 65:10)
All you men of Egypt, Goshen, Pathros and all their inhabitants! The king has commanded us to build Pithom and Rameses, and to fortify them for battle; who among you of all Egypt, of the children of Israel and of all the inhabitants of the cities, are willing to build with us, shall each have his wages given to him daily at the king's order; so go you first and do cunningly, and gather yourselves and come to Pithom and Rameses to build.

(Jasher 65:11)
And while you are building, cause a proclamation of this kind to be made throughout Egypt every day at the command of the king.

(Jasher 65:12)
And when some of the children of Israel shall come to build with you, you shall give them their wages daily for a few days.

(Jasher 65:13)
And after they shall have built with you for their daily hire, drag yourselves away from them daily one by one in secret, and then you shall rise up and become their task-masters and officers, and you shall leave them afterward to build without wages, and should they refuse, then force them with all your might to build.

(Jasher 65:14)
And if you do this it will be well with us to strengthen our land against the children of Israel, for on account of the fatigue of the building and the work, the children of Israel will decrease, because you will deprive them from their wives day by day.

(Jasher 65:15)
And all the elders of Egypt heard the counsel of the king, and the counsel seemed good in their eyes and in the eyes of the servants of Pharaoh, and in the eyes of all Egypt, and they did according to the word of the king.

(Jasher 65:16)
And all the servants went away from the king, and they caused a proclamation to be made in all Egypt, in Tachpanches and in Goshen, and in all the cities which surrounded Egypt, saying,

(Jasher 65:17)
You have seen what the children of Esau and Ishmael did to us, who came to war against us and wished to destroy us.

(Jasher 65:18)
Now therefore the king commanded us to fortify the land, to build the cities Pithom and Rameses, and to fortify them for battle, if they should again come against us.

(Jasher 65:19)
Whosoever of you from all Egypt and from the children of Israel will come to build with us, he shall have his daily wages given by the king, as his command is to us.

(Jasher 65:20)
And when Egypt and all the children of Israel heard all that the servants of Pharaoh had spoken, there came from the Egyptians, and the children of Israel to build with the servants of Pharaoh, Pithom and Rameses, but none of the children of Levi came with their brethren to build.

(Jasher 65:21)
And all the servants of Pharaoh and his princes came at first

Book Six: From Goshen to Sinai

with deceit to build with all Israel as daily hired laborers, and they gave to Israel their daily hire at the beginning.

(Jasher 65:22)
And the servants of Pharaoh built with all Israel, and were employed in that work with Israel for a month.

(Jasher 65:23)
And at the end of the month, all the servants of Pharaoh began to withdraw secretly from the people of Israel daily.

(Jasher 65:24)
And Israel went on with the work at that time, but they then received their daily hire, because some of the men of Egypt were yet carrying on the work with Israel at that time; therefore the Egyptians gave Israel their hire in those days, in order that they, the Egyptians their fellow-workmen, might also take the pay for their labor.

(Jasher 65:25)
And at the end of a year and four months all the Egyptians had withdrawn from the children of Israel, so that the children of Israel were left alone engaged in the work.

(Exodus 1:11...) (Jasher 65:26) (Jubilees 46:14...)
Therefore after all the Egyptians had withdrawn from the children of Israel they returned and became oppressors and officers over them, and some of them stood over the children of Israel as task masters to receive from them all that they gave them for the pay of their labor; they set over them taskmasters to afflict them with slavery with their burdens.

(Jasher 65:27)
And the Egyptians did in this manner to the children of Israel

day by day, in order to afflict in their work.

(Jasher 65:28)
And all the children of Israel were alone engaged in the labor, and the Egyptians refrained from giving any pay to the children of Israel from that time forward.

(Jasher 65:29)
And when some of the men of Israel refused to work on account of the wages not being given to them, then the exactors and the servants of Pharaoh oppressed them and smote them with heavy blows, and made them return by force, to labor with their brethren; thus did all the Egyptians to the children of Israel all the days.

(Jasher 65:30)
And all the children of Israel were greatly afraid of the Egyptians in this matter, and all the children of Israel returned and worked alone without pay.

(...Exodus 1:11) (Jasher 65:31) (...Jubilees 46:14)
And the children of Israel built for Pharaoh strong treasure cities, Pithom and Raamses, and all the children of Israel did the work, some making bricks, and some building, and the children of Israel built and fortified all the land of Egypt and its walls which had fallen in the cities of Egypt. And the children of Israel were engaged in work for many years, until the time came when the Lord remembered them and brought them out of Egypt.

(Exodus 1:12) (Jubilees 46:15...)
But the more they afflicted them, the more they multiplied and grew. And they were grieved because of the children of Israel.

Book Six: From Goshen to Sinai

(Jasher 65:32)
But the children of Levi were not employed in the work with their brothers of Israel, from the beginning to the day of their going forth from Egypt.

(Jasher 65:33)
For all the children of Levi knew that the Egyptians had spoken all these words with deceit to the Israelites, therefore the children of Levi refrained from approaching to the work with their brothers.

(Jasher 65:34)
And the Egyptians did not direct their attention to make the children of Levi work afterward, since they had not been with their brothers at the beginning, therefore the Egyptians left them alone.

(Exodus 1:13) (Jasher 65:35) (...Jubilees 46:15)
And the hands of the men of Egypt were directed with continued severity against the children of Israel in that work, and the Egyptians made the children of Israel to serve with rigor:

(Jubilees 46:15)
And the people of Egypt abominated the children of Israel.

(Exodus 1:14) (Jasher 65:36)
And the Egyptians made their lives bitter with hard bondage, in mortar, and in brick, and in all manner of service in the field: all their service, wherein they made them serve, was with rigor.

(Jasher 65:37)
And the children of Israel called Melol the king of Egypt

"Meror, king of Egypt," because in his days the Egyptians had embittered their lives with all manner of work.

(Jasher 65:38)
And all the work wherein the Egyptians made the children of Israel labor, they exacted with rigor, in order to afflict the children of Israel, but the more they afflicted them, the more they increased and grew, and the Egyptians were grieved because of the children of Israel.

~ ~ ~

(Jasher 66:1)
At that time died Hadad the son of Bedad king of Edom, and Samlah from Mesrekah, from the country of the children of the east, reigned in his place.

(Jasher 66:2)
In the thirteenth year of the reign of Pharaoh king of Egypt, which was the hundred and twenty-fifth year of the Israelites going down into Egypt, Samlah had reigned over Edom eighteen years.

(Jasher 66:3)
And when he reigned, he drew forth his hosts to go and fight against Zepho the son of Eliphaz and the children of Chittim, because they had made war against Angeas king of Africa, and they destroyed his whole army.

(Jasher 66:4)
But he did not engage with him, for the children of Esau prevented him, saying, He was their brother, so Samlah

listened to the voice of the children of Esau, and turned back with all his forces to the land of Edom, and did not proceed to fight against Zepho the son of Eliphaz.

(Jasher 66:5)
And Pharaoh king of Egypt heard this thing, saying, Samlah king of Edom has resolved to fight the children of Chittim, and afterward he will come to fight against Egypt.

(Jasher 66:6)
And when the Egyptians heard this matter, they increased the labor upon the children of Israel, lest the Israelites should do to them as they did to them in their war with the children of Esau in the days of Hadad.

(Jasher 66:7)
So the Egyptians said to the children of Israel, Hasten and do your work, and finish your task, and strengthen the land, lest the children of Esau your brothers should come to fight against us, for on your account will they come against us.

(Jasher 66:8)
And the children of Israel did the work of the men of Egypt day by day, and the Egyptians afflicted the children of Israel in order to lessen them in the land.

(Jasher 66:9)
But as the Egyptians increased the labor upon the children of Israel, so did the children of Israel increase and multiply, and all Egypt was filled with the children of Israel.

(Jasher 66:10)
And in the hundred and twenty-fifth year of Israel's going down into Egypt, all the Egyptians saw that their counsel did

not succeed against Israel, but that they increased and grew, and the land of Egypt and the land of Goshen were filled with the children of Israel.

(Jasher 66:11)
So all the elders of Egypt and its wise men came before the king and bowed down to him and sat before him.

(Jasher 66:12)
And all the elders of Egypt and the wise men thereof said to the king, May the king live forever; you counseled us the counsel against the children of Israel, and we did to them according to the word of the king.

(Jasher 66:13)
But in proportion to the increase of the labor so do they increase and grow in the land, and behold the whole country is filled with them.

(Jasher 66:14)
Now therefore our lord and king, the eyes of all Egypt are upon you to give them advice with your wisdom, by which they may prevail over Israel to destroy them, or to diminish them from the land; and the king answered them saying, Give you counsel in this matter that we may know what to do to them.

(Jasher 66:15)
And an officer, one of the king's counselors, whose name was Job, from Mesopotamia, in the land of Uz, answered the king, saying,

(Jasher 66:16)
If it please the king, let him hear the counsel of his servant;

Book Six: From Goshen to Sinai

and the king said to him, Speak.

(Jasher 66:17)
And Job spoke before the king, the princes, and before all the elders of Egypt, saying,

(Jasher 66:18)
Behold the counsel of the king which he advised formerly respecting the labor of the children of Israel is very good, and you must not remove from them that labor forever.

(Jasher 66:19)
But this is the advice counseled by which you may lessen them, if it seems good to the king to afflict them.

(Jasher 66:20)
Behold we have feared war for a long time, and we said, When Israel becomes fruitful in the land, they will drive us from the land if a war should take place.

(Jasher 66:21)
If it please the king, let a royal decree go forth, and let it be written in the laws of Egypt which shall not be revoked, that every male child born to the Israelites, his blood shall be spilled upon the ground.

(Jasher 66:22)
And by your doing this, when all the male children of Israel shall have died, the evil of their wars will cease; let the king do so and send for all the Hebrew midwives and order them in this matter to execute it; so the thing pleased the king and the princes, and the king did according to the word of Job.

(Jasher 66:23...)
And the king sent for the Hebrew midwives to be called.

(Jasher 66:24)
And the midwives came before the king, and stood in his presence.

(Exodus 1:15) (...Jasher 66:23)
And the king of Egypt spoke to the Hebrew midwives, of which the name of the one was Shiphrah, and the name of the other Puah:

(Exodus 1:16) (Jasher 66:25)
And he said to them, When you do the office of a midwife to the Hebrew women, and see them upon the stools; if it be a son, then you shall kill him: but if it be a daughter, then she shall live.

(Jasher 66:26)
But if you will not do this thing, then will I burn you up and all your houses with fire.

(Exodus 1:17) (Jasher 66:27)
But the midwives feared God, and did not as the king of Egypt commanded them, but saved the men children alive. And when the Hebrew women brought forth to the midwife son or daughter, then did the midwife do all that was necessary to the child and let it live; thus did the midwives all the days.

(Exodus 1:18) (Jasher 66:28)
And this thing was told to the king, and the king of Egypt sent and called for the midwives, and said to them, Why have you done this thing, and have saved the men children alive?

Book Six: From Goshen to Sinai

(Exodus 1:19) (Jasher 66:29, 30)
　　And together the midwives said to Pharaoh, Let not the king think that the Hebrew women are as the Egyptian women; because the Hebrew women are not as the Egyptian women; for all the children of Israel are lively / hale, and are delivered ere the midwives come in to them. And as for us your handmaids, for many days no Hebrew woman has brought forth upon us, for all the Hebrew women are their own midwives, because they are hale.

(Exodus 1:20) (Jasher 66:31)
　　And Pharaoh heard their words and believed them in this matter, and the midwives went away from the king. Therefore God dealt well with the midwives: and the people multiplied, and waxed very mighty.

(Exodus 1:21)
　　And it came to pass, because the midwives feared God, that he made them houses.

～ ～ ～

(Jasher 67:1)
There was a man in the land of Egypt of the seed of Levi, whose name was Amram, the son of Kehath, the son of Levi, the son of Israel.

(Jasher 67:2)
And this man went and took a wife, namely Jochebed the daughter of Levi his father's sister, and she was one hundred and twenty-six years old, and he came to her.

(Jasher 67:3)
And the woman conceived and bare a daughter, and she called her name Miriam, because in those days the Egyptians had embittered the lives of the children of Israel.

(Jasher 67:4)
And she conceived again and bare a son and she called his name Aaron, for in the days of her conception, Pharaoh began to spill the blood of the male children of Israel.

(Jasher 67:5)
In those days died Zepho the son of Eliphaz, son of Esau, king of Chittim, and Janeas reigned in his stead.

(Jasher 67:6)
And the time that Zepho reigned over the children of Chittim was fifty years, and he died and was buried in the city of Nabna in the land of Chittim.

(Jasher 67:7)
And Janeas, one of the mighty men of the children of Chittim, reigned after him and he reigned fifty years.

(Jasher 67:8)
And it was after the death of the king of Chittim that Balaam the son of Beor fled from the land of Chittim, and he went and came to Egypt to Pharaoh king of Egypt.

(Jasher 67:9)
And Pharaoh received him with great honor, for he had heard of his wisdom, and he gave him presents and made him for a counselor, and aggrandized him.

Book Six: From Goshen to Sinai

(Jasher 67:10)
And Balaam dwelt in Egypt, in honor with all the nobles of the king, and the nobles exalted him, because they all coveted to learn his wisdom.

(Jasher 67:11)
And in the hundred and thirtieth year of Israel's going down to Egypt, Pharaoh dreamed that he was sitting upon his kingly throne, and lifted up his eyes and saw an old man standing before him, and there were scales in the hands of the old man, such scales as are used by merchants.

(Jasher 67:12)
And the old man took the scales and hung them before Pharaoh.

(Jasher 67:13)
And the old man took all the elders of Egypt and all its nobles and great men, and he tied them together and put them in one scale.

(Jasher 67:14)
And he took a milk kid and put it into the other scale, and the kid preponderated over all.

(Jasher 67:15)
And Pharaoh was astonished at this dreadful vision, why the kid should preponderate over all, and Pharaoh awoke and behold it was a dream.

(Jasher 67:16)
And Pharaoh rose up early in the morning and called all his servants and related to them the dream, and the men were greatly afraid.

(Jasher 67:17)
And the king said to all his wise men, Interpret I pray you the dream which I dreamed, that I may know it.

(Jasher 67:18)
And Balaam the son of Beor answered the king and said to him, This means nothing else but a great evil that will spring up against Egypt in the latter days.

(Jasher 67:19)
For a son will be born to Israel who will destroy all Egypt and its inhabitants, and bring forth the Israelites from Egypt with a mighty hand.

(Jasher 67:20)
Now therefore, O king, take counsel upon this matter, that you may destroy the hope of the children of Israel and their expectation, before this evil arise against Egypt.

(Jasher 67:21)
And the king said to Balaam, And what shall we do to Israel? Surely after a certain manner did we at first counsel against them and could not prevail over them.

(Jasher 67:22)
Now therefore give you also advice against them by which we may prevail over them.

(Jasher 67:23)
And Balaam answered the king, saying, Send now and call your two counselors, and we will see what their advice is upon this matter and afterward your servant will speak.

(Jasher 67:24)
And the king sent and called his two counselors Reuel the Midianite and Job the Uzite, and they came and sat before the king.

(Jasher 67:25)
And the king said to them, Behold you have both heard the dream which I have dreamed, and the interpretation thereof; now therefore give counsel and know and see what is to be done to the children of Israel, whereby we may prevail over them, before their evil shall spring up against us.

(Jasher 67:26)
And Reuel the Midianite answered the king and said, May the king live, may the king live forever.

(Jasher 67:27)
If it seem good to the king, let him desist from the Hebrews and leave them, and let him not stretch forth his hand against them.

(Jasher 67:28)
For these are they whom the Lord chose in days of old, and took as the lot of his inheritance from among all the nations of the earth and the kings of the earth; and who is there that stretched his hand against them with impunity, of whom their God was not avenged?

(Jasher 67:29)
Surely you know that when Abraham went down to Egypt, Pharaoh, the former king of Egypt, saw Sarah his wife, and took her for a wife, because Abraham said, She is my sister, for he was afraid, lest the men of Egypt should slay him on account of his wife.

(Jasher 67:30)
And when the king of Egypt had taken Sarah then God smote him and his household with heavy plagues, until he restored to Abraham his wife Sarah, then was he healed.

(Jasher 67:31)
And Abimelech the Gerarite, king of the Philistines, God punished on account of Sarah wife of Abraham, in stopping up every womb from man to beast.

(Jasher 67:32)
When their God came to Abimelech in the dream of night and terrified him in order that he might restore to Abraham Sarah whom he had taken, and afterward all the people of Gerar were punished on account of Sarah, and Abraham prayed to his God for them, and he was entreated of him, and he healed them.

(Jasher 67:33)
And Abimelech feared all this evil that came upon him and his people, and he returned to Abraham his wife Sarah, and gave him with her many gifts.

(Jasher 67:34)
He did so also to Isaac when he had driven him from Gerar, and God had done wonderful things to him, that all the water courses of Gerar were dried up, and their productive trees did not bring forth.

(Jasher 67:35)
Until Abimelech of Gerar, and Ahuzzath one of his friends, and Pichol the captain of his host, went to him and they bent and bowed down before him to the ground.

Book Six: From Goshen to Sinai

(Jasher 67:36)
And they requested of him to supplicate for them, and he prayed to the Lord for them, and the Lord was entreated of him and he healed them.

(Jasher 67:37)
Jacob also, the plain man, was delivered through his integrity from the hand of his brother Esau, and the hand of Laban the Syrian his mother's brother, who had sought his life; likewise from the hand of all the kings of Canaan who had come together against him and his children to destroy them, and the Lord delivered them out of their hands, that they turned upon them and smote them, for who had ever stretched forth his hand against them with impunity?

(Jasher 67:38)
Surely Pharaoh the former, your father's father, raised Joseph the son of Jacob above all the princes of the land of Egypt, when he saw his wisdom, for through his wisdom he rescued all the inhabitants of the land from the famine.

(Jasher 67:39)
After which he ordered Jacob and his children to come down to Egypt, in order that through their virtue, the land of Egypt and the land of Goshen might be delivered from the famine.

(Jasher 67:40)
Now therefore if it seems good in your eyes, cease from destroying the children of Israel, but if it be not your will that they shall dwell in Egypt, send them forth from here, that they may go to the land of Canaan, the land where their ancestors sojourned.

(Jasher 67:41)
And when Pharaoh heard the words of Jethro he was very angry with him, so that he rose with shame from the king's presence, and went to Midian, his land, and took Joseph's stick with him.

(Jasher 67:42)
And the king said to Job the Uzite, What do you say Job, and what is your advice respecting the Hebrews?

(Jasher 67:43)
So Job said to the king, Behold all the inhabitants of the land are in your power, let the king do as it seems good in his eyes.

(Jasher 67:44)
And the king said to Balaam, What do you say, Balaam, speak your word that we may hear it.

(Jasher 67:45)
And Balaam said to the king, Of all that the king has counseled against the Hebrews will they be delivered, and the king will not be able to prevail over them with any counsel.

(Jasher 67:46)
For if you think to lessen them by the flaming fire, you can not prevail over them, for surely their God delivered Abraham their father from Ur of the Chaldeans; and if you think to destroy them with a sword, surely Isaac their father was delivered from it, and a ram was placed in his stead.

(Jasher 67:47)
And if with hard and rigorous labor you think to lessen them, you will not prevail even in this, for their father Jacob served Laban in all manner of hard work, and prospered.

(Jasher 67:48)
Now therefore, O King, hear my words, for this is the counsel which is counseled against them, by which you will prevail over them, and from which you should not depart.

(Jasher 67:49)
If it please the king let him order all their children which shall be born from this day forward, to be thrown into the water, for by this can you wipe away their name, for none of them, nor of their fathers, were tried in this manner.

(Jasher 67:50)
And the king heard the words of Balaam, and the thing pleased the king and the princes, and the king did according to the word of Balaam.

(Jasher 67:51)
And the king ordered a proclamation to be issued and a law to be made throughout the land of Egypt, saying, Every male child born to the Hebrews from this day forward shall be thrown into the water.

(Exodus 1:22) (Jasher 67:52)
And Pharaoh called to all his servants, saying, Go now and seek throughout the land of Goshen where the children of Israel are, and he charged all his people, saying, See that every son that is born to the Hebrews you shall cast into the river, and every daughter you shall save alive.

(Jasher 67:53)
And when the children of Israel heard this thing which Pharaoh had commanded, to cast their male children into the river, some of the people separated from their wives and others adhered to them.

(Jasher 67:54)
And from that day forward, when the time of delivery arrived to those women of Israel who had remained with their husbands, they went to the field to bring forth there, and they brought forth in the field, and left their children upon the field and returned home.

(Jasher 67:55)
And the Lord who had sworn to their ancestors to multiply them, sent one of his ministering angels which are in heaven to wash each child in water, to anoint and swathe it and to put into its hands two smooth stones from one of which it sucked milk and from the other honey, and he caused its hair to grow to its knees, by which it might cover itself; to comfort it and to cleave to it, through his compassion for it.

(Jasher 67:56)
And when God had compassion over them and had desired to multiply them upon the face of the land, he ordered his earth to receive them to be preserved therein till the time of their growing up, after which the earth opened its mouth and vomited them forth and they sprouted forth from the city like the herb of the earth, and the grass of the forest, and they returned each to his family and to his father's house, and they remained with them.

(Jasher 67:57)
And the babes of the children of Israel were upon the earth like the herb of the field, through God's grace to them.

(Jasher 67:58)
And when all the Egyptians saw this thing, they went forth, each to his field with his yoke of oxen and his plowshare, and they plowed it up as one plows the earth at seed time.

Book Six: From Goshen to Sinai

(Jasher 67:59)
And when they plowed they were unable to hurt the infants of the children of Israel, so the people increased and waxed exceedingly.

(Jasher 67:60)
And Pharaoh ordered his officers daily to go to Goshen to seek for the babes of the children of Israel.

(Jasher 67:61)
And when they had sought and found one, they took it from its mother's bosom by force, and threw it into the river, but the female child they left with its mother; thus did the Egyptians do to the Israelites all the days.

The History of Ancient Israel

Exodus: Chapter Two

(Exodus 2:1)
And there went a man of the house of Levi, and took to wife a daughter of Levi.

(Jasher 68:1)
And it was at that time the spirit of God was upon Miriam the daughter of Amram the sister of Aaron, and she went forth and prophesied about the house, saying, Behold a son will be born to us from my father and mother this time, and he will save Israel from the hands of Egypt.

(Jasher 68:2) (Jubilees 47:1...)
And in the seventh week, in the seventh year, in the forty-seventh jubilee, when Amram heard the words of his daughter, he went forth from the land of Canaan, and took his wife back to the house, after he had driven her away at the time when Pharaoh ordered every male child of the house of Jacob to be thrown into the water.

(Exodus 2:2...) (Jasher 68:3)
So Amram took Jochebed his wife, three years after he had driven her away, and he came to her and the woman conceived.

(...Exodus 2:2...) (Jasher 68:4) (...Jubilees 47:1)
And at the end of seven months from her conception she bore a son in the fourth week, in the sixth year thereof, in the forty-eighth jubilee: and the whole house was filled with great

light as of the light of the sun and moon at the time of their shining. This was the time of tribulation on the children of Israel.

(Jubilees 47:2)
And Pharaoh, king of Egypt, issued a command regarding them that they should cast all their male children which were born into the river.

(Jubilees 47:3)
And they cast them in for seven months until the day that Moses was born.

(...Exodus 2:2) (Jasher 68:5) (Jubilees 47:4...)
And when the woman saw him that he was a goodly child, and pleasing to the sight, she hid him three months in an inner room.

(Jasher 68:6)
In those days the Egyptians conspired to destroy all the Hebrews there.

(Jasher 68:7)
And the Egyptian women went to Goshen where the children of Israel were, and they carried their young ones upon their shoulders, their babes who could not yet speak.

(Jasher 68:8)
And in those days, when the women of the children of Israel brought forth, each woman had hidden her son from before the Egyptians, that the Egyptians might not know of their bringing forth, and might not destroy them from the land.

Book Six: From Goshen to Sinai

(Jasher 68:9)
And the Egyptian women came to Goshen and their children who could not speak were upon their shoulders, and when an Egyptian woman came into the house of a Hebrew woman her babe began to cry.

(Jasher 68:10) (...Jubilees 47:4...)
And when it cried the child that was in the inner room answered it, so the Egyptian women went and they told it regarding her at the house of Pharaoh.

(Jasher 68:11)
And Pharaoh sent his officers to take the children and slay them; thus did the Egyptians to the Hebrew women all the days.

(Jasher 68:12)
And it was at that time, about three months from Jochebed's concealment of her son, that the thing was known in Pharaoh's house.

(Exodus 2:3) (Jasher 68:13) (...Jubilees 47:4)
And the woman hastened when she could not longer hide him to take away her son before the officers came, and she took for him an ark of bulrushes, and daubed it with slime and with pitch, and put the child therein; and she laid it in the flags by the river's brink seven days, and his mother came by night and suckled him, and by day Miriam, his sister, guarded him from the birds.

(Exodus 2:4) (Jasher 68:14)
And his sister Miriam stood afar off, to know what would be done to him, and what would become of her words.

(Jasher 68:15)
And God sent forth at that time a terrible heat in the land of Egypt, which burned up the flesh of man like the sun in his circuit, and it greatly oppressed the Egyptians.

(Jasher 68:16)
And all the Egyptians went down to bathe in the river, on account of the consuming heat which burned up their flesh.

(Exodus 2:5...) (Jasher 68:17) (Jubilees 47:5...)
And in those days Bathia / Tharmuth, the daughter of Pharaoh also came down to wash herself at the river, owing to the consuming heat, and her maidens walked along by the river's side, and all the women of Egypt as well.

(...Exodus 2:5) (Jasher 68:18) (...Jubilees 47:5...)
And she heard his voice crying, and Bathia lifted up her eyes to the river and when she saw the ark upon the water among the flags, she sent her maids to fetch it and they brought it to her.

(Exodus 2:6) (Jasher 68:19) (Jubilees 47:6)
And when she had opened it, she saw the child: and, behold, the babe wept. And she took you out of the ark, and she had compassion on him, and said, This is one of the Hebrews' children.

(Jasher 68:20)
And all the women of Egypt walking on the river side desired to give him suck, but he would not suck, for this thing was from the Lord, in order to restore him to his mother's breast.

(Exodus 2:7) (Jasher 68:21) (Jubilees 47:7)
And Miriam his sister was at that time among the Egyptian

women at the river side, and she saw this thing then she said to Pharaoh's daughter, Shall I go and call to you a nurse of the Hebrew women, that she may nurse and suckle the child for you?

(Exodus 2:8) (Jasher 68:22) (Jubilees 47:8...)
And Pharaoh's daughter said to her, Go. And the maid went and called Jochebed, the child's mother.

(Exodus 2:9) (Jasher 68:23)
And Pharaoh's daughter said to Jochebed, Take this child away, and nurse it for me, and I will give you your wages, two bits of silver daily. And the woman took the child, and nursed it.

(...Jubilees 47:8)
And she gave her wages, and she nursed him.

(Exodus 2:10) (Jasher 68:24) (Jubilees 47:9)
And at the end of two years, when the child grew up, she brought him to Pharaoh's daughter, and he became her son. And she called his name Moses: and she said, Because I drew him out of the water. And Amram your father taught you writing, and after you had completed three weeks they brought you into the royal court.

(Jasher 68:25)
And Amram his father called his name Chabar, for he said, It was for him that he associated with his wife whom he had turned away.

(Jasher 68:26)
And Jochebed his mother called his name Jekuthiel, Because,

she said, I have hoped for him to the Almighty, and God restored him to me.

(Jasher 68:27)
And Miriam his sister called him Jered, for she descended after him to the river to know what his end would be.

(Jasher 68:28)
And Aaron his brother called his name Abi Zanuch, saying, My father left my mother and returned to her on his account.

(Jasher 68:29)
And Kehath the father of Amram called his name Abigdor, because on his account did God repair the breach of the house of Jacob, that they could no longer throw their male children into the water.

(Jasher 68:30)
And their nurse called him Abi Socho, saying, In his tabernacle was he hidden for three months, on account of the children of Ham.

(Jasher 68:31)
And all Israel called his name Shemaiah, son of Nethanel, for they said, In his days has God heard their cries and rescued them from their oppressors.

(Jasher 68:32)
And Moses was in Pharaoh's house, and was to Bathia, Pharaoh's daughter, as a son, and Moses grew up among the king's children.

~ ~ ~

Book Six: From Goshen to Sinai

(Jasher 69:1)
And the king of Edom died in those days, in the eighteenth year of his reign, and was buried in his temple which he had built for himself as his royal residence in the land of Edom.

(Jasher 69:2)
And the children of Esau sent to Pethor, which is upon the river, and they fetched from there a young man of beautiful eyes and comely aspect, whose name was Saul, and they made him king over them in the place of Samlah.

(Jasher 69:3)
And Saul reigned over all the children of Esau in the land of Edom for forty years.

(Jasher 69:4)
And when Pharaoh king of Egypt saw that the counsel which Balaam had advised respecting the children of Israel did not succeed, but that still they were fruitful, multiplied and increased throughout the land of Egypt,

(Jasher 69:5)
Then Pharaoh commanded in those days that a proclamation should be issued throughout Egypt to the children of Israel, saying, No man shall diminish any thing of his daily labor.

(Jasher 69:6)
And the man who shall be found deficient in his labor which he performs daily, whether in mortar or in bricks, then his youngest son shall be put in their place.

(Jasher 69:7)
And the labor of Egypt strengthened upon the children of Israel in those days, and behold if one brick was deficient in any man's daily labor, the Egyptians took his youngest boy by

force from his mother, and put him into the building in the place of the brick which his father had left wanting.

(Jasher 69:8)
And the men of Egypt did so to all the children of Israel day by day, all the days for a long period.

(Jasher 69:9)
But the tribe of Levi did not at that time work with the Israelites their brothers, from the beginning, for the children of Levi knew the cunning of the Egyptians which they exercised at first toward the Israelites.

~ ~ ~

(Jasher 70:1)
And in the third year from the birth of Moses, Pharaoh was sitting at a banquet, when Alparanith the queen was sitting at his right and Bathia at his left, and the lad Moses was lying upon her bosom, and Balaam the son of Beor with his two sons, and all the princes of the kingdom were sitting at table in the king's presence.

(Jasher 70:2)
And the lad stretched forth his hand upon the king's head, and took the crown from the king's head and placed it on his own head.

(Jasher 70:3)
And when the king and princes saw the work which the boy had done, the king and princes were terrified, and one man to his neighbor expressed astonishment.

Book Six: From Goshen to Sinai

(Jasher 70:4)
And the king said to the princes who were before him at table, What do you speak and what do you say, O you princes, in this matter, and what is to be the judgment against the boy on account of this act?

(Jasher 70:5)
And Balaam the son of Beor the magician answered before the king and princes, and he said, Remember now, O my lord and king, the dream which you did dream many days since, and that which your servant interpreted to you.

(Jasher 70:6)
Now therefore this is a child from the Hebrew children, in whom is the spirit of God, and let not my lord the king imagine that this youngster did this thing without knowledge.

(Jasher 70:7)
For he is a Hebrew boy, and wisdom and understanding are with him, although he is yet a child, and with wisdom has he done this and chosen to himself the kingdom of Egypt.

(Jasher 70:8)
For this is the manner of all the Hebrews to deceive kings and their nobles, to do all these things cunningly, in order to make the kings of the earth and their men tremble.

(Jasher 70:9)
Surely you know that Abraham their father acted thus, who deceived the army of Nimrod king of Babel, and Abimelech king of Gerar, and that he possessed himself of the land of the children of Heth and all the kingdoms of Canaan.

(Jasher 70:10)
And that he descended into Egypt and said of Sarah his wife, she is my sister, in order to mislead Egypt and her king.

(Jasher 70:11)
His son Isaac also did so when he went to Gerar and dwelt there, and his strength prevailed over the army of Abimelech king of the Philistines.

(Jasher 70:12)
He also thought of making the kingdom of the Philistines stumble, in saying that Rebecca his wife was his sister.

(Jasher 70:13)
Jacob also dealt treacherously with his brother, and took from his hand his birthright and his blessing.

(Jasher 70:14)
He went then to Padan-aram to the house of Laban his mother's brother, and cunningly obtained from him his daughter, his cattle, and all belonging to him, and fled away and returned to the land of Canaan to his father.

(Jasher 70:15)
His sons sold their brother Joseph, who went down into Egypt and became a slave, and was placed in the prison house for twelve years.

(Jasher 70:16)
Until the former Pharaoh dreamed dreams, and withdrew him from the prison house, and magnified him above all the princes in Egypt on account of his interpreting his dreams to him.

(Jasher 70:17)
And when God caused a famine throughout the land he sent for and brought his father and all his brothers, and the whole of his father's household, and supported them without price or reward, and bought the Egyptians for slaves.

(Jasher 70:18)
Now therefore my lord king behold this child has risen up in their stead in Egypt, to do according to their deeds and to trifle with every king, prince and judge.

(Jasher 70:19)
If it please the king, let us now spill his blood upon the ground, lest he grow up and take away the government from your hand, and the hope of Egypt perish after he shall have reigned.

(Jasher 70:20)
And Balaam said to the king, Let us moreover call for all the judges of Egypt and the wise men thereof, and let us know if the judgment of death is due to this boy as you said, and then we will slay him.

(Jasher 70:21)
And Pharaoh sent and called for all the wise men of Egypt and they came before the king, and an angel of the Lord came among them, and he was like one of the wise men of Egypt.

(Jasher 70:22)
And the king said to the wise men, Surely you have heard what this Hebrew boy who is in the house has done, and thus has Balaam judged in the matter.

(Jasher 70:23)
Now judge you also and see what is due to the boy for the act he has committed.

(Jasher 70:24)
And the angel, who seemed like one of the wise men of Pharaoh, answered and said as follows, before all the wise men of Egypt and before the king and the princes:

(Jasher 70:25)
If it please the king let the king send for men who shall bring before him an onyx stone and a coal of fire, and place them before the child, and if the child shall stretch forth his hand and take the onyx stone, then shall we know that with wisdom has the youth done all that he has done, and we must slay him.

(Jasher 70:26)
But if he stretch forth his hand upon the coal, then shall we know that it was not with knowledge that he did this thing, and he shall live.

(Jasher 70:27)
And the thing seemed good in the eyes of the king and the princes, so the king did according to the word of the angel of the Lord.

(Jasher 70:28)
And the king ordered the onyx stone and coal to be brought and placed before Moses.

(Jasher 70:29)
And they placed the boy before them, and the lad endeavored to stretch forth his hand to the onyx stone, but the angel of the Lord took his hand and placed it upon the coal, and the coal

Book Six: From Goshen to Sinai

became extinguished in his hand, and he lifted it up and put it into his mouth, and burned part of his lips and part of his tongue, and he became heavy in mouth and tongue.

(Jasher 70:30)
And when the king and princes saw this, they knew that Moses had not acted with wisdom in taking off the crown from the king's head.

(Jasher 70:31)
So the king and princes refrained from slaying the child, so Moses remained in Pharaoh's house, growing up, and the Lord was with him.

(Jasher 70:32)
And while the boy was in the king's house, he was robed in purple and he grew among the children of the king.

(Jasher 70:33)
And when Moses grew up in the king's house, Bathia the daughter of Pharaoh considered him as a son, and all the household of Pharaoh honored him, and all the men of Egypt were afraid of him.

(Exodus 2:11...) (Jasher 70:34)
And it came to pass in those days, when Moses was grown, that he daily went forth and came into the land of Goshen, where his brethren the children of Israel were, and looked on their burdens and Moses saw them daily in shortness of breath and hard labor:

(Jasher 70:35)
And Moses asked them, saying, Wherefore is this labor meted out to you day by day?

(Jasher 70:36)
And they told him all that had befallen them, and all the injunctions which Pharaoh had put upon them before his birth.

(Jasher 70:37)
And they told him all the counsels which Balaam the son of Beor had counseled against them, and what he had also counseled against him in order to slay him when he had taken the king's crown from off his head.

(Jasher 70:38)
And when Moses heard these things his anger was kindled against Balaam, and he sought to kill him, and he was in ambush for him day by day.

(Jasher 70:39)
And Balaam was afraid of Moses, and he and his two sons rose up and went forth from Egypt, and they fled and delivered their souls and betook themselves to the land of Cush to Kikianus, king of Cush.

(Jasher 70:40)
And Moses was in the king's house going out and coming in, the Lord gave him favor in the eyes of Pharaoh, and in the eyes of all his servants, and in the eyes of all the people of Egypt, and they loved Moses exceedingly.

(Jasher 70:41)
And the day arrived when Moses went to Goshen to see his brothers, that he saw the children of Israel in their burdens and hard labor, and Moses was grieved on their account.

Book Six: From Goshen to Sinai

(Jasher 70:42)
And Moses returned to Egypt and came to the house of Pharaoh, and came before the king, and Moses bowed down before the king.

(Jasher 70:43)
And Moses said to Pharaoh, I pray you my lord, I have come to seek a small request from you, turn not away my face empty; and Pharaoh said to him, Speak.

(Jasher 70:44)
And Moses said to Pharaoh, Let there be given to your servants the children of Israel who are in Goshen, one day to rest therein from their labor.

(Jasher 70:45)
And the king answered Moses and said, Behold I have lifted up your face in this thing to grant your request.

(Jasher 70:46)
And Pharaoh ordered a proclamation to be issued throughout Egypt and Goshen, saying,

(Jasher 70:47)
To you, all the children of Israel, thus says the king, for six days you shall do your work and labor, but on the seventh day you shall rest, and shall not preform any work, thus shall you do all the days, as the king and Moses the son of Bathia have commanded.

(Jasher 70:48)
And Moses rejoiced at this thing which the king had granted to him, and all the children of Israel did as Moses ordered them.

(Jasher 70:49)
For this thing was from the Lord to the children of Israel, for the Lord had begun to remember the children of Israel to save them for the sake of their fathers.

(Jasher 70:50)
And the Lord was with Moses and his fame went throughout Egypt.

(Jasher 70:51)
And Moses became great in the eyes of all the Egyptians, and in the eyes of all the children of Israel, seeking good for his people Israel and speaking words of peace regarding them to the king.

(...Exodus 2:11) (Jasher 71:1) (Jubilees 47:10...)
And Moses was three weeks of years at court until the time when he went forth from the royal court. And when Moses was eighteen years old, he desired to see his father and mother and he went to them to Goshen, and when Moses had come near Goshen, he came to the place where the children of Israel were engaged in work, and he observed their burdens, and he spied an Egyptian smiting his friend who was of the children of Israel, a Hebrew, one of his brethren.

(Jasher 71:2)
And when the man who was beaten saw Moses he ran to him for help, for the man Moses was greatly respected in the house of Pharaoh, and he said to him, My lord attend to me, this Egyptian came to my house in the night, bound me, and came to my wife in my presence, and now he seeks to take my life away.

Book Six: From Goshen to Sinai

(Exodus 2:12) (Jasher 71:3) (...Jubilees 47:10)
And when Moses heard this wicked thing, his anger was kindled against the Egyptian, and he looked this way and that way, and when he saw that there was no man, he slew the Egyptian, and hid him in the sand, and delivered the Hebrew from the hand of him that smote him.

(Jasher 71:4)
And the Hebrew went to his house, and Moses returned to his home, and went forth and came back to the king's house.

(Jasher 71:5)
And when the man had returned home, he thought of repudiating his wife, for it was not right in the house of Jacob, for any man to come to his wife after she had been defiled.

(Jasher 71:6)
And the woman went and told her brothers, and the woman's brothers sought to slay him, and he fled to his house and escaped.

(Exodus 2:13) (Jasher 71:7) (Jubilees 47:11)
And when he went out the second day, behold, two men of the Hebrews strove together: and he said to him that did the wrong, Why do you smite your fellow?

(Exodus 2:14) (Jasher 71:8) (Jubilees 47:12)
And he was angry and indignant and said, Who made you a prince and a judge over us? Do you intend to kill me, as you killed the Egyptian? And Moses feared and fled on account of these words, and said, Surely this thing is known.

(Exodus 2:15...) (Jasher 71:9)
Now when Pharaoh heard this thing, he sought to slay Moses

and he ordered Moses to be slain, so God sent his angel, and he appeared to Pharaoh in the likeness of a captain of the guard.

(Jasher 71:10)
And the angel of the Lord took the sword from the hand of the captain of the guard, and took his head off with it, for the likeness of the captain of the guard was turned into the likeness of Moses.

(...Exodus 2:15...) (Jasher 71:11)
And the angel of the Lord took hold of the right hand of Moses, and brought him forth from Egypt, and placed him from without the borders of Egypt, a distance of forty days' journey. And Moses fled from the face of Pharaoh.

(Jubilees 48:1...)
And in the sixth year of the third week of the forty-ninth jubilee, he departed and dwelt in the land of Midian, five weeks and one year.

(Jasher 71:12)
And Aaron his brother alone remained in the land of Egypt, and he prophesied to the children of Israel, saying,

(Jasher 71:13)
Thus says the Lord God of your ancestors, Throw away, each man, the abominations of his eyes, and do not defile yourselves with the idols of Egypt.

(Jasher 71:14)
And the children of Israel rebelled and would not hearken to Aaron at that time.

Book Six: From Goshen to Sinai

(Jasher 71:15)
And the Lord thought to destroy them, were it not that the Lord remembered the covenant which he had made with Abraham, Isaac and Jacob.

(Jasher 71:16)
In those days the hand of Pharaoh continued to be severe against the children of Israel, and he crushed and oppressed them until the time when God sent forth his word and took notice of them.

~ ~ ~

(Jasher 72:1)
And it was in those days that there was a great war between the children of Cush and the children of the east and Aram, and they rebelled against the king of Cush in whose hands they were.

(Jasher 72:2)
So Kikianus king of Cush went forth with all the children of Cush, a people numerous as the sand, and he went to fight against Aram and the children of the east, to bring them under subjection.

(Jasher 72:3)
And when Kikianus went out, he left Balaam the magician, with his two sons, to guard the city, and the lowest sort of the people of the land.

(Jasher 72:4)
So Kikianus went forth to Aram and the children of the east,

and he fought against them and smote them, and they all fell down wounded before Kikianus and his people.

(Jasher 72:5)
And he took many of them captives and he brought them under subjection as at first, and he encamped upon their land to take tribute from them as usual.

(Jasher 72:6)
And Balaam the son of Beor, when the king of Cush had left him to guard the city and the poor of the city, he rose up and advised with the people of the land to rebel against king Kikianus, not to let him enter the city when he should come home.

(Jasher 72:7)
And the people of the land hearkened to him, and they swore to him and made him king over them, and his two sons for captains of the army.

(Jasher 72:8)
So they rose up and raised the walls of the city at the two corners, and they built an exceeding strong building.

(Jasher 72:9)
And at the third corner they dug ditches without number, between the city and the river which surrounded the whole land of Cush, and they made the waters of the river burst forth there.

(Jasher 72:10)
At the fourth corner they collected numerous serpents by their incantations and enchantments, and they fortified the city and dwelt therein, and no one went out or in before them.

(Jasher 72:11)
And Kikianus fought against Aram and the children of the east and he subdued them as before, and they gave him their usual tribute, and he went and returned to his land.

(Jasher 72:12)
And when Kikianus the king of Cush approached his city and all the captains of the forces with him, they lifted up their eyes and saw that the walls of the city were built up and greatly elevated, so the men were astonished at this.

(Jasher 72:13)
And they said one to the other, It is because they saw that we were delayed, in battle, and were greatly afraid of us, therefore have they done this thing and raised the city walls and fortified them so that the kings of Canaan might not come in battle against them.

(Jasher 72:14)
So the king and the troops approached the city door and they looked up and behold, all the gates of the city were closed, and they called out to the sentinels, saying, Open to us, that we may enter the city.

(Jasher 72:15)
But the sentinels refused to open to them by the order of Balaam the magician, their king, they suffered them not to enter their city.

(Jasher 72:16)
So they raised a battle with them opposite the city gate, and one hundred and thirty men of the army at Kikianus fell on that day.

(Jasher 72:17)
And on the next day they continued to fight and they fought at the side of the river; they endeavored to pass but were not able, so some of them sank in the pits and died.

(Jasher 72:18)
So the king ordered them to cut down trees to make rafts, upon which they might pass to them, and they did so.

(Jasher 72:19)
And when they came to the place of the ditches, the waters revolved by mills, and two hundred men upon ten rafts were drowned.

(Jasher 72:2)
And on the third day they came to fight at the side where the serpents were, but they could not approach there, for the serpents slew of them one hundred and seventy men, and they ceased fighting against Cush, and they besieged Cush for nine years, no person came out or in.

(Jasher 72:21)
At that time that the war and the siege were against Cush, Moses fled from Egypt from Pharaoh who sought to kill him for having slain the Egyptian.

(Jasher 72:22)
And Moses was eighteen years old when he fled from Egypt from the presence of Pharaoh, and he fled and escaped to the camp of Kikianus, which at that time was besieging Cush.

(Jasher 72:23)
And Moses was nine years in the camp of Kikianus king of Cush, all the time that they were besieging Cush, and Moses

Book Six: From Goshen to Sinai

went out and came in with them.

(Jasher 72:24)
And the king and princes and all the fighting men loved Moses, for he was great and worthy, his stature was like a noble lion, his face was like the sun, and his strength was like that of a lion, and he was counselor to the king.

(Jasher 72:25)
And at the end of nine years, Kikianus was seized with a mortal disease, and his illness prevailed over him, and he died on the seventh day.

(Jasher 72:26)
So his servants embalmed him and carried him and buried him opposite the city gate to the north of the land of Egypt.

(Jasher 72:27)
And they built over him an elegant strong and high building, and they placed great stones below.

(Jasher 72:28)
And the king's scribes engraved upon those stones all the might of their king Kikianus, and all his battles which he had fought, behold they are written there at this day.

(Jasher 72:29)
Now after the death of Kikianus king of Cush it grieved his men and troops greatly on account of the war.

(Jasher 72:3)
So they said one to the other, Give us counsel what we are to do at this time, as we have resided in the wilderness nine years away from our homes.

(Jasher 72:31)
If we say we will fight against the city many of us will fall wounded or killed, and if we remain here in the siege we shall also die.

(Jasher 72:32)
For now all the kings of Aram and of the children of the east will hear that our king is dead, and they will attack us suddenly in a hostile manner, and they will fight against us and leave no remnant of us.

(Jasher 72:33)
Now therefore let us go and make a king over us, and let us remain in the siege until the city is delivered up to us.

(Jasher 72:34)
And they wished to choose on that day a man for king from the army of Kikianus, and they found no object of their choice like Moses to reign over them.

(Jasher 72:35)
And they hastened and stripped off each man his garments and cast them upon the ground, and they made a great heap and placed Moses thereon.

(Jasher 72:36)
And they rose up and blew with trumpets and called out before him, and said, May the king live, may the king live!

(Jasher 72:37)
And all the people and nobles swore to him to give him for a wife Adoniah the queen, the Cushite, wife of Kikianus, and they made Moses king over them on that day.

(Jasher 72:38)
And all the people of Cush issued a proclamation on that day, saying, Every man must give something to Moses of what is in his possession.

(Jasher 72:39)
And they spread out a sheet upon the heap, and every man cast into it something of what he had, one a gold earring and the other a coin.

(Jasher 72:40)
Also of onyx stones, bdellium, pearls and marble did the children of Cush cast to Moses upon the heap, also silver and gold in great abundance.

(Jasher 72:41)
And Moses took all the silver and gold, all the vessels, and the bdellium and onyx stones, which all the children of Cush had given to him, and he placed them among his treasures.

(Jasher 72:42)
And Moses reigned over the children of Cush on that day, in the place of Kikianus king of Cush.

~ ~ ~

(Jasher 73:1)
In the fifty-fifth year of the reign of Pharaoh king of Egypt, that is in the hundred and fifty-seventh year of the Israelites going down into Egypt, reigned Moses in Cush.

(Jasher 73:2)
Moses was twenty-seven years old when he began to reign over Cush, and forty years did he reign.

(Jasher 73:3)
And the Lord granted Moses favor and grace in the eyes of all the children of Cush, and the children of Cush loved him exceedingly, so Moses was favored by the Lord and by men.

(Jasher 73:4)
And in the seventh day of his reign, all the children of Cush assembled and came before Moses and bowed down to him to the ground.

(Jasher 73:5)
And all the children spoke together in the presence of the king, saying, Give us counsel that we may see what is to be done to this city.

(Jasher 73:6)
For it is now nine years that we have been besieging round about the city, and have not seen our children and our wives.

(Jasher 73:7)
So the king answered them, saying, If you will hearken to my voice in all that I shall command you, then will the Lord give the city into our hands and we shall subdue it.

(Jasher 73:8)
For if we fight with them as in the former battle which we had with them before the death of Kikianus, many of us will fall down wounded as before.

Book Six: From Goshen to Sinai

(Jasher 73:9)
Now therefore behold here is counsel for you in this matter; if you will hearken to my voice, then will the city be delivered into our hands.

(Jasher 73:10)
So all the forces answered the king, saying, All that our lord shall command that will we do.

(Jasher 73:11)
And Moses said to them, Pass through and proclaim a voice in the whole camp to all the people, saying,

(Jasher 73:12)
Thus says the king, Go into the forest and bring with you of the young ones of the stork, each man a young one in his hand.

(Jasher 73:13)
And any person transgressing the word of the king, who shall not bring his young one, he shall die, and the king will take all belonging to him.

(Jasher 73:14)
And when you shall bring them they shall be in your keeping, you shall rear them until they grow up, and you shall teach them to dart upon, as is the way of the young ones of the hawk.

(Jasher 73:15)
So all the children of Cush heard the words of Moses, and they rose up and caused a proclamation to be issued throughout the camp, saying,

(Jasher 73:16)
To you, all the children of Cush, the king's order is, that you

go all together to the forest, and catch there the young storks each man his young one in his hand, and you shall bring them home.

(Jasher 73:17)
And any person violating the order of the king shall die, and the king will take all that belongs to him.

(Jasher 73:18)
And all the people did so, and they went out to the wood and they climbed the fir trees and caught, each man a young one in his hand, all the young of the storks, and they brought them into the desert and reared them by order of the king, and they taught them to dart upon, similar to the young hawks.

(Jasher 73:19)
And after the young storks were reared, the king ordered them to be hungered for three days, and all the people did so.

(Jasher 73:20)
And on the third day, the king said to them, strengthen yourselves and become valiant men, and put on each man his armor and gird on his sword upon him, and ride each man his horse and take each his young stork in his hand.

(Jasher 73:21)
And we will rise up and fight against the city at the place where the serpents are; and all the people did as the king had ordered.

(Jasher 73:22)
And they took each man his young one in his hand, and they went away, and when they came to the place of the serpents

the king said to them, Send forth each man his young stork upon the serpents.

(Jasher 73:23)
And they sent forth each man his young stork at the king's order, and the young storks ran upon the serpents and they devoured them all and destroyed them out of that place.

(Jasher 73:24)
And when the king and people had seen that all the serpents were destroyed in that place, all the people set up a great shout.

(Jasher 73:25)
And they approached and fought against the city and took it and subdued it, and they entered the city.

(Jasher 73:26)
And there died on that day one thousand and one hundred men of the people of the city, all that inhabited the city, but of the people besieging not one died.

(Jasher 73:27)
So all the children of Cush went each to his home, to his wife and children and to all belonging to him.

(Jasher 73:28)
And Balaam the magician, when he saw that the city was taken, he opened the gate and he and his two sons and eight brothers fled and returned to Egypt to Pharaoh king of Egypt.

(Jasher 73:29)
They are the sorcerers and magicians who are mentioned in the book of the law, standing against Moses when the Lord

brought the plagues upon Egypt.

(Jasher 73:30)
So Moses took the city by his wisdom, and the children of Cush placed him on the throne instead of Kikianus king of Cush.

(Jasher 73:31)
And they placed the royal crown upon his head, and they gave him for a wife Adoniah the Cushite queen, wife of Kikianus.

(Jasher 73:32)
And Moses feared the Lord God of his fathers, so that he came not to her, nor did he turn his eyes to her.

(Jasher 73:33)
For Moses remembered how Abraham had made his servant Eliezer swear, saying to him, You shall not take a woman from the daughters of Canaan for my son Isaac.

(Jasher 73:34)
Also what Isaac did when Jacob had fled from his brother, when he commanded him, saying, You shall not take a wife from the daughters of Canaan, nor make alliance with any of the children of Ham.

(Jasher 73:35)
For the Lord our God gave Ham the son of Noah, and his children and all his seed, as slaves to the children of Shem and to the children of Japheth, and to their seed after them for slaves, forever.

(Jasher 73:36)
Therefore Moses turned not his heart nor his eyes to the wife

of Kikianus all the days that he reigned over Cush.

(Jasher 73:37)
And Moses feared the Lord his God all his life, and Moses walked before the Lord in truth, with all his heart and soul, he turned not from the right way all the days of his life; he declined not from the way either to the right or to the left, in which Abraham, Isaac and Jacob had walked.

(Jasher 73:38)
And Moses strengthened himself in the kingdom of the children of Cush, and he guided the children of Cush with his usual wisdom, and Moses prospered in his kingdom.

(Jasher 73:39)
And at that time Aram and the children of the east heard that Kikianus king of Cush had died, so Aram and the children of the east rebelled against Cush in those days.

(Jasher 73:40)
And Moses gathered all the children of Cush, a people very mighty, about thirty thousand men, and he went forth to fight with Aram and the children of the east.

(Jasher 73:41)
And they went at first to the children of the east, and when the children of the east heard their report, they went to meet them, and engaged in battle with them.

(Jasher 73:42)
And the war was severe against the children of the east, so the Lord gave all the children of the east into the hand of Moses, and about three hundred men fell down slain.

(Jasher 73:43)
And all the children of the east turned back and retreated, so Moses and the children of Cush followed them and subdued them, and put a tax upon them, as was their custom.

(Jasher 73:44)
So Moses and all the people with him passed from there to the land of Aram for battle.

(Jasher 73:45)
And the people of Aram also went to meet them, and they fought against them, and the Lord delivered them into the hand of Moses, and many of the men of Aram fell down wounded.

(Jasher 73:46)
And Aram also were subdued by Moses and the people of Cush, and also gave their usual tax.

(Jasher 73:47)
And Moses brought Aram and the children of the east under subjection to the children of Cush, and Moses and all the people who were with him, turned to the land of Cush.

(Jasher 73:48)
And Moses strengthened himself in the kingdom of the children of Cush, and the Lord was with him, and all the children of Cush were afraid of him.

~ ~ ~

(Jasher 74:1)
In the end of years died Saul king of Edom, and Baal Chanan the son of Achbor reigned in his place.

(Jasher 74:2)
In the sixteenth year of the reign of Moses over Cush, Baal Chanan the son of Achbor reigned in the land of Edom over all the children of Edom for thirty-eight years.

(Jasher 74:3)
In his days Moab rebelled against the power of Edom, having been under Edom since the days of Hadad the son of Bedad, who smote them and Midian, and brought Moab under subjection to Edom.

(Jasher 74:4)
And when Baal Chanan the son of Achbor reigned over Edom, all the children of Moab withdrew their allegiance from Edom.

(Jasher 74:5)
And Angeas king of Africa died in those days, and Azdrubal his son reigned in his stead.

(Jasher 74:6)
And in those days died Janeas king of the children of Chittim, and they buried him in his temple which he had built for himself in the plain of Canopia for a residence, and Latinus reigned in his stead.

(Jasher 74:7)
In the twenty-second year of the reign of Moses over the children of Cush, Latinus reigned over the children of Chittim forty-five years.

(Jasher 74:8)
And he also built for himself a great and mighty tower, and he built therein an elegant temple for his residence, to conduct his government, as was the custom.

(Jasher 74:9)
In the third year of his reign he caused a proclamation to be made to all his skilful men, who made many ships for him.

(Jasher 74:10)
And Latinus assembled all his forces, and they came in ships, and went therein to fight with Azdrubal son of Angeas king of Africa, and they came to Africa and engaged in battle with Azdrubal and his army.

(Jasher 74:11)
And Latinus prevailed over Azdrubal, and Latinus took from Azdrubal the aqueduct which his father had brought from the children of Chittim, when he took Janiah the daughter of Uzi for a wife, so Latinus overthrew the bridge of the aqueduct, and smote the whole army of Azdrubal a severe blow.

(Jasher 74:12)
And the remaining strong men of Azdrubal strengthened themselves, and their hearts were filled with envy, and they courted death, and again engaged in battle with Latinus king of Chittim.

(Jasher 74:13)
And the battle was severe upon all the men of Africa, and they all fell wounded before Latinus and his people, and Azdrubal the king also fell in that battle. And the king Azdrubal had a very beautiful daughter, whose name was Ushpezena, and all the men of Africa embroidered her likeness on their garments, on account of her great beauty and comely appearance.

Book Six: From Goshen to Sinai

(Jasher 74:14)
And the men of Latinus saw Ushpezena, the daughter of Azdrubal, and praised her to Latinus their king.

(Jasher 74:15)
And Latinus ordered her to be brought to him, and Latinus took Ushpezena for a wife, and he turned back on his way to Chittim.

(Jasher 74:16)
And it was after the death of Azdrubal son of Angeas, when Latinus had turned back to his land from the battle, that all the inhabitants of Africa rose up and took Anibal the son of Angeas, the younger brother of Azdrubal, and made him king instead at his brother over the whole land at Africa.

(Jasher 74:17)
And when he reigned, he resolved to go to Chittim to fight with the children of Chittim, to avenge the cause of Azdrubal his brother, and the cause of the inhabitants of Africa, and he did so.

(Jasher 74:18)
And he made many ships, and he came therein with his whole army, and he went to Chittim.

(Jasher 74:19)
So Anibal fought with the children of Chittim, and the children of Chittim fell wounded before Anibal and his army, and Anibal avenged his brother's cause.

(Jasher 74:20)
And Anibal continued the war for eighteen years with the children of Chittim, and Anibal dwelt in the land of Chittim and encamped there for a long time.

(Jasher 74:21)
And Anibal smote the children of Chittim very severely, and he slew their great men and princes, and of the rest of the people he smote about eighty thousand men.

(Jasher 74:22)
And at the end of days and years, Anibal returned to his land of Africa, and he reigned securely in the place of Azdrubal his brother.

(Jasher 75:1)
At that time, in the hundred and eightieth year of the Israelites going down into Egypt, there went forth from Egypt valiant men, thirty thousand on foot, from the children of Israel, who were all of the tribe of Joseph, of the children of Ephraim the son of Joseph.

(Jasher 75:2)
For they said the period was completed which the Lord had appointed to the children of Israel in the times of old, which he had spoken to Abraham.

(Jasher 75:3)
And these men girded themselves, and they put each man his sword at his side, and every man his armor upon him, and they trusted to their strength, and they went out together from Egypt with a mighty hand.

(Jasher 75:4)
But they brought no provision for the road, only silver and gold, not even bread for that day did they bring in their hands, for they thought of getting their provision for pay from the Philistines, and if not they would take it by force.

(Jasher 75:5)
And these men were very mighty and valiant men, one man could pursue a thousand and two could rout ten thousand, so they trusted to their strength and went together as they were.

(Jasher 75:6)
And they directed their course toward the land of Gath, and they went down and found the shepherds of Gath feeding the cattle of the children of Gath.

(Jasher 75:7)
And they said to the shepherds, Give us some of the sheep for pay, that we may eat, for we are hungry, for we have eaten no bread this day.

(Jasher 75:8)
And the shepherds said, Are they our sheep or cattle that we should give them to you even for pay? So the children of Ephraim approached to take them by force.

(Jasher 75:9)
And the shepherds of Gath shouted over them that their cry was heard at a distance, so all the children of Gath went out to them.

(Jasher 75:10)
And when the children of Gath saw the evil doings of the children of Ephraim, they returned and assembled the men of Gath, and they put on each man his armor, and came forth to the children of Ephraim for battle.

(Jasher 75:11)
And they engaged with them in the valley of Gath, and the battle was severe, and they smote from each other a great many on that day.

(Jasher 75:12)
And on the second day the children of Gath sent to all the cities of the Philistines that they should come to their help, saying,

(Jasher 75:13)
Come up to us and help us, that we may smite the children of Ephraim who have come forth from Egypt to take our cattle, and to fight against us without cause.

(Jasher 75:14)
Now the souls of the children of Ephraim were exhausted with hunger and thirst, for they had eaten no bread for three days. And forty thousand men went forth from the cities of the Philistines to the assistance of the men of Gath.

(Jasher 75:15)
And these men were engaged in battle with the children of Ephraim, and the Lord delivered the children of Ephraim into the hands of the Philistines.

(Jasher 75:16)
And they smote all the children of Ephraim, all who had gone forth from Egypt, none were remaining but ten men who had run away from the engagement.

(Jasher 75:17)
For this evil was from the Lord against the children of Ephraim, for they transgressed the word of the Lord in going forth from Egypt, before the period had arrived which the Lord in the days of old had appointed to Israel.

(Jasher 75:18)
And of the Philistines also there fell a great many, about

Book Six: From Goshen to Sinai

twenty thousand men, and their brothers carried them and buried them in their cities.

(Jasher 75:19)
And the slain of the children of Ephraim remained forsaken in the valley of Gath for many days and years, and were not brought to burial, and the valley was filled with men's bones.

(Jasher 75:20)
And the men who had escaped from the battle came to Egypt, and told all the children of Israel all that had befallen them.

(Jasher 75:21)
And their father Ephraim mourned over them for many days, and his brothers came to console him.

(Jasher 75:22)
And he came to his wife and she bare a son, and he called his name Beriah, for she was unfortunate in his house.

~ ~ ~

(Jasher 76:1)
And Moses the son of Amram was still king in the land of Cush in those days, and he prospered in his kingdom, and he conducted the government of the children of Cush in justice, in righteousness, and integrity.

(Jasher 76:2)
And all the children of Cush loved Moses all the days that he reigned over them, and all the inhabitants of the land of Cush were greatly afraid of him.

(Jasher 76:3)
And in the fortieth year of the reign of Moses over Cush, Moses was sitting on the royal throne while Adoniah the queen was before him, and all the nobles were sitting around him.

(Jasher 76:4)
And Adoniah the queen said before the king and the princes, What is this thing which you, the children of Cush, have done for this long time?

(Jasher 76:5)
Surely you know that for forty years that this man has reigned over Cush he has not approached me, nor has he served the gods of the children of Cush.

(Jasher 76:6)
Now therefore hear, O you children of Cush, and let this man no more reign over you as he is not of our flesh.

(Jasher 76:7)
Behold Menacrus my son is grown up, let him reign over you, for it is better for you to serve the son of your lord, than to serve a stranger, slave of the king of Egypt.

(Jasher 76:8)
And all the people and nobles of the children of Cush heard the words which Adoniah the queen had spoken in their ears.

(Jasher 76:9)
And all the people were preparing until the evening, and in the morning they rose up early and made Menacrus, son of Kikianus, king over them.

(Jasher 76:10)
And all the children of Cush were afraid to stretch forth their hand against Moses, for the Lord was with Moses, and the children of Cush remembered the oath which they swore to Moses, therefore they did no harm to him.

(Jasher 76:11)
But the children of Cush gave many presents to Moses, and sent him from them with great honor.

(Jasher 76:12)
So Moses went forth from the land of Cush, and went home and ceased to reign over Cush, and Moses was sixty-six years old when he went out of the land of Cush, for the thing was from the Lord, for the period had arrived which he had appointed in the days of old, to bring forth Israel from the affliction of the children of Ham.

(...Exodus 2:15) (Jasher 76:13)
So Moses went to Midian, for he was afraid to return to Egypt on account of Pharaoh, and he went and dwelt in the land of Midian: and he sat down by a well of water in Midian.

(Exodus 2:16) (Jasher 76:14, 15)
Now the priest of Midian, Reuel the Midianite had seven daughters: went out to feed their father's flock, and they came to the well and drew water, and filled the troughs to water their father's flock.

(Exodus 2:17) (Jasher 76:16)
And the shepherds came and drove them away: but Moses stood up and helped them, and watered their flock.

(Exodus 2:18) (Jasher 76:17)
And when they came to Reuel their father, he said, How is it that you are come so soon today? And they told him what Moses did for them.

(Exodus 2:19) (Jasher 76:18)
And they said, An Egyptian delivered us out of the hand of the shepherds, and also drew water enough for us, and watered the flock.

(Exodus 2:20) (Jasher 76:19)
And he said to his daughters, And where is he? Why is it that you have left the man? Call him, that he may eat bread.

(Jasher 76:20)
And Reuel sent for him and fetched him and brought him home, and he ate bread with him.

(Jasher 76:21)
And Moses related to Reuel that he had fled from Egypt and that he reigned forty years over Cush, and that they afterward had taken the government from him, and had sent him away in peace with honor and with presents.

(Jasher 76:22)
And when Reuel had heard the words of Moses, Reuel said within himself, I will put this man into the prison house, whereby I shall conciliate the children of Cush, for he has fled from them.

(Jasher 76:23)
And they took and put him into the prison house, and Moses was in prison ten years, and while Moses was in the prison house, Zipporah the daughter of Reuel took pity over him,

and supported him with bread and water all the time.

(Jasher 77:26)
And Moses the son of Amram was still confined in the dungeon in those days, in the house of Reuel the Midianite, and Zipporah the daughter of Reuel did support him with food secretly day by day.

(Jasher 77:27)
And Moses was confined in the dungeon in the house of Reuel for ten years.

(Jasher 77:28)
And at the end of ten years which was the first year of the reign of Pharaoh over Egypt, in the place of his father,

(Jasher 77:29)
Zipporah said to her father Reuel, No person inquires or seeks after the Hebrew man, whom you did bind in prison now ten years.

(Jasher 77:30)
Now therefore, if it seems good in your sight, let us send and see whether he is living or dead, but her father knew not that she had supported him.

(Jasher 77:31)
And Reuel her father answered and said to her, Has ever such a thing happened that a man should be shut up in a prison without food for ten years, and that he should live?

(Jasher 77:32)
And Zipporah answered her father, saying, Surely you have

heard that the God of the Hebrews is great and awful, and does wonders for them at all times.

(Jasher 77:33)
He it was who delivered Abraham from Ur of the Chaldeans, and Isaac from the sword of his father, and Jacob from the angel of the Lord who wrestled with him at the ford of Jabbuk.

(Jasher 77:34)
Also with this man has he done many things, he delivered him from the river in Egypt and from the sword of Pharaoh, and from the children of Cush, so also can he deliver him from famine and make him live.

(Jasher 77:35)
And the thing seemed good in the sight of Reuel, and he did according to the word of his daughter, and sent to the dungeon to ascertain what became of Moses.

(Jasher 77:36)
And he saw, and behold the man Moses was living in the dungeon, standing upon his feet, praising and praying to the God of his ancestors.

(Jasher 77:37)
And Reuel commanded Moses to be brought out of the dungeon, so they shaved him and he changed his prison garments and ate bread.

(Jasher 77:38)
And afterward Moses went into the garden of Reuel which was behind the house, and he there prayed to the Lord his God, who had done mighty wonders for him.

(Jasher 77:39)
And it was that while he prayed he looked opposite to him, and behold a sapphire stick was placed in the ground, which was planted in the midst of the garden.

(Jasher 77:40)
And he approached the stick and he looked, and behold the name of the Lord God of hosts was engraved thereon, written and developed upon the stick.

(Jasher 77:41)
And he read it and stretched forth his hand and he plucked it like a forest tree from the thicket, and the stick was in his hand.

(Jasher 77:42)
And this is the stick with which all the works of our God were performed, after he had created heaven and earth, and all the host of them, seas, rivers and all their fishes.

(Jasher 77:43)
And when God had driven Adam from the garden of Eden, he took the stick in his hand and went and tilled the ground from which he was taken.

(Jasher 77:44)
And the stick came down to Noah and was given to Shem and his descendants, until it came into the hand of Abraham the Hebrew.

(Jasher 77:45)
And when Abraham had given all he had to his son Isaac, he also gave to him this stick.

(Jasher 77:46)
And when Jacob had fled to Padan-aram, he took it into his hand, and when he returned to his father he had not left it behind him.

(Jasher 77:47)
Also when he went down to Egypt he took it into his hand and gave it to Joseph, one portion above his brothers, for Jacob had taken it by force from his brother Esau.

(Jasher 77:48)
And after the death of Joseph, the nobles of Egypt came into the house of Joseph, and the stick came into the hand of Reuel the Midianite, and when he went out of Egypt, he took it in his hand and planted it in his garden.

(Jasher 77:49)
And all the mighty men of the Kinites tried to pluck it when they endeavored to get Zipporah his daughter, but they were unsuccessful.

(Jasher 77:50)
So that stick remained planted in the garden of Reuel, until he came who had a right to it and took it.

(Exodus 2:21...)
And Moses was content to dwell with the man:

~ ~ ~

(Jasher 78:1)
At that time died Baal Channan son of Achbor, king of Edom, and was buried in his house in the land of Edom.

(Jasher 78:2)
And after his death the children of Esau sent to the land of Edom, and took from there a man who was in Edom, whose name was Hadad, and they made him king over them in the place of Baal Channan, their king.

(Jasher 78:3)
And Hadad reigned over the children of Edom forty-eight years.

(Jasher 78:4)
And when he reigned he resolved to fight against the children of Moab, to bring them under the power of the children of Esau as they were before, but he was not able, because the children of Moab heard this thing, and they rose up and hastened to elect a king over them from among their brothers.

(Jasher 78:5)
And they afterward gathered together a great people, and sent to the children of Ammon their brothers for help to fight against Hadad king of Edom.

(Jasher 78:6)
And Hadad heard the thing which the children of Moab had done, and was greatly afraid of them, and refrained from fighting against them.

(...Exodus 2:21) (Jasher 77:51)
And when Reuel saw the stick in the hand of Moses, he

wondered at it, and he gave Moses Zipporah his daughter for a wife.

(Jasher 78:7)
In those days Moses, the son of Amram, in Midian, took Zipporah, the daughter of Reuel the Midianite, for a wife.

(Jasher 78:8)
And Zipporah walked in the ways of the daughters of Jacob, she was nothing short of the righteousness of Sarah, Rebecca, Rachel and Leah.

(Exodus 2:22) (Jasher 78:9)
And Zipporah conceived and she bore him a son, and he called his name Gershom: for he said, I have been a stranger in a strange land; but he circumcised not his foreskin, at the command of Reuel his father-in-law.

(Jasher 78:10)
And she conceived again and bare a son, but circumcised his foreskin, and called his name Eliezer, for Moses said, Because the God of my fathers was my help, and delivered me from the sword of Pharaoh.

~ ~ ~

(Jasher 76:24)
And all the children of Israel were yet in the land of Egypt serving the Egyptians in all manner of hard work, and the hand of Egypt continued in severity over the children of Israel in those days.

(Jasher 76:25)
At that time the Lord smote Pharaoh king of Egypt, and he afflicted with the plague of leprosy from the sole of his foot to the crown of his head; owing to the cruel treatment of the children of Israel was this plague at that time from the Lord upon Pharaoh king of Egypt.

(Jasher 76:26)
For the Lord had hearkened to the prayer of his people the children of Israel, and their cry reached him on account of their hard work.

(Jasher 76:27)
Still his anger did not turn from them, and the hand of Pharaoh was still stretched out against the children of Israel, and Pharaoh hardened his neck before the Lord, and he increased his yoke over the children of Israel, and embittered their lives with all manner of hard work.

(Jasher 76:28)
And when the Lord had inflicted the plague upon Pharaoh king of Egypt, he asked his wise men and sorcerers to cure him.

(Jasher 76:29)
And his wise men and sorcerers said to him, That if the blood of little children were put into the wounds he would be healed.

(Jasher 76:30)
And Pharaoh hearkened to them, and sent his ministers to Goshen to the children of Israel to take their little children.

(Jasher 76:31)
And Pharaoh's ministers went and took the infants of the

children of Israel from the bosoms of their mothers by force, and they brought them to Pharaoh daily, a child each day, and the physicians killed them and applied them to the plague; thus did they all the days.

(Jasher 76:32)
And the number of the children which Pharaoh slew was three hundred and seventy-five.

(Jasher 76:33)
But the Lord hearkened not to the physicians of the king of Egypt, and the plague went on increasing mightily.

(Jasher 76:34)
And Pharaoh was ten years afflicted with that plague, still the heart of Pharaoh was more hardened against the children of Israel.

(Jasher 76:35)
And at the end of ten years the Lord continued to afflict Pharaoh with destructive plagues.

(Jasher 76:36)
And the Lord smote him with a bad tumor and sickness at the stomach, and that plague turned to a severe boil.

(Jasher 76:37)
At that time the two ministers of Pharaoh came from the land of Goshen where all the children of Israel were, and went to the house of Pharaoh and said to him, We have seen the children of Israel slacken in their work and negligent in their labor.

(Jasher 76:38)
And when Pharaoh heard the words of his ministers, his anger was kindled against the children of Israel exceedingly, for he was greatly grieved at his bodily pain.

(Jasher 76:39)
And he answered and said, Now that the children of Israel know that I am ill, they turn and scoff at us, now therefore harness my chariot for me, and I will betake myself to Goshen and will see the scoff of the children of Israel with which they are deriding me; so his servants harnessed the chariot for him.

(Jasher 76:40)
And they took and made him ride upon a horse, for he was not able to ride of himself;

(Jasher 76:41)
And he took with him ten horsemen and ten footmen, and went to the children of Israel to Goshen.

(Jasher 76:42)
And when they had come to the border of Egypt, the king's horse passed into a narrow place, elevated in the hollow part of the vineyard, fenced on both sides, the low, plain country being on the other side.

(Jasher 76:43)
And the horses ran rapidly in that place and pressed each other, and the other horses pressed the king's horse.

(Jasher 76:44)
And the king's horse fell into the low plain while the king was riding upon it, and when he fell the chariot turned over the

king's face and the horse lay upon the king, and the king cried out, for his flesh was very sore.

(Jasher 76:45)
And the flesh of the king was torn from him, and his bones were broken and he could not ride, for this thing was from the Lord to him, for the Lord had heard the cries of his people the children of Israel and their affliction.

(Jasher 76:46)
And his servants carried him upon their shoulders, a little at a time, and they brought him back to Egypt, and the horsemen who were with him came also back to Egypt.

(Jasher 76:47)
And they placed him in his bed, and the king knew that his end was come to die, so Aparanith the queen his wife came and cried before the king, and the king wept a great weeping with her.

(Jasher 76:48)
And all his nobles and servants came on that day and saw the king in that affliction, and wept a great weeping with him.

(Jasher 76:49)
And the princes of the king and all his counselors advised the king to cause one to reign in his stead in the land, whomsoever he should choose from his sons.

(Jasher 76:50)
And the king had three sons and two daughters which Aparanith the queen his wife had borne to him, besides the king's children of concubines.

(Jasher 76:51)
And these were their names, the firstborn Othri, the second Adikam, and the third Morion, and their sisters, the name of the elder Bathia and of the other Acuzi.

(Jasher 76:52)
And Othri the first born of the king was an idiot, precipitate and hurried in his words.

(Jasher 76:53)
But Adikam was a cunning and wise man and knowing in all the wisdom of Egypt, but of unseemly aspect, thick in flesh, and very short in stature; his height was one cubit.

(Jasher 76:54)
And when the king saw Adikam his son intelligent and wise in all things, the king resolved that he should be king in his stead after his death.

(Jasher 76:55)
And he took for him a wife Gedudah daughter of Abilot, and he was ten years old, and she bare to him four sons.

(Jasher 76:56)
And he afterward went and took three wives and begot eight sons and three daughters.

(Jasher 76:57)
And the disorder greatly prevailed over the king, and his flesh stank like the flesh of a carcass cast upon the field in summer time, during the heat of the sun.

(Jasher 76:58)
And when the king saw that his sickness had greatly

strengthened itself over him, he ordered his son Adikam to be brought to him, and they made him king over the land in his place.

(Exodus 2:23...) (Jasher 76:59)
And it came to pass in process of time, at the end of three years, that the king of Egypt died, in shame, disgrace, and disgust, and his servants carried him and buried him in the sepulcher of the kings of Egypt in Zoan Mizraim.

(Jasher 76:60)
But they embalmed him not as was usual with kings, for his flesh was putrid, and they could not approach to embalm him on account of the stench, so they buried him in haste.

(Jasher 76:61)
For this evil was from the Lord to him, for the Lord had requited him evil for the evil which in his days he had done to Israel.

(Jasher 76:62)
And he died with terror and with shame, and his son Adikam reigned in his place.

~ ~ ~

(Jasher 77:1)
Adikam was twenty years old when he reigned over Egypt, he reigned four years.

Book Six: From Goshen to Sinai

(Jasher 77:2)
In the two hundred and sixth year of Israel's going down to Egypt did Adikam reign over Egypt, but he continued not so long in his reign over Egypt as his fathers had continued their reigns.

(Jasher 77:3)
For Melol his father reigned ninety-four years in Egypt, but he was ten years sick and died, for he had been wicked before the Lord.

(Jasher 77:4)
And all the Egyptians called the name of Adikam Pharaoh like the name of his fathers, as was their custom to do in Egypt.

(Jasher 77:5)
And all the wise men of Pharaoh called the name of Adikam Ahuz, for short is called Ahuz in the Egyptian language.

(Jasher 77:6)
And Adikam was exceedingly ugly, and he was a cubit and a span and he had a great beard which reached to the soles of his feet.

(Jasher 77:7)
And Pharaoh sat upon his father's throne to reign over Egypt, and he conducted the government of Egypt in his wisdom.

(Jasher 77:8)
And while he reigned he exceeded his father and all the preceding kings in wickedness, and he increased his yoke over the children of Israel.

(Jasher 77:9)
And he went with his servants to Goshen to the children of Israel, and he strengthened the labor over them and he said to them, Complete your work, each day's task, and let not your hands slacken from our work from this day forward as you did in the days of my father.

(Jasher 77:10)
And he placed officers over them from among the children of Israel, and over these officers he placed taskmasters from among his servants.

(Jasher 77:11)
And he placed over them a measure of bricks for them to do according to that number, day by day, and he turned back and went to Egypt.

(Jasher 77:12)
At that time the task-masters of Pharaoh ordered the officers of the children of Israel according to the command of Pharaoh, saying,

(Jasher 77:13)
Thus says Pharaoh, Do your work each day, and finish your task, and observe the daily measure of bricks; diminish not anything.

(Jasher 77:14)
And it shall come to pass that if you are deficient in your daily bricks, I will put your young children in their stead.

(Jasher 77:15)
And the task-masters of Egypt did so in those days as Pharaoh had ordered them.

(Jasher 77:16)
And whenever any deficiency was found in the children of Israel's measure of their daily bricks, the task-masters of Pharaoh would go to the wives of the children of Israel and take infants of the children of Israel to the number of bricks deficient, they would take them by force from their mother's laps, and put them in the building instead of the bricks;

(Jasher 77:17)
While their fathers and mothers were crying over them and weeping when they heard the weeping voices of their infants in the wall of the building.

(Jasher 77:18)
And the task-masters prevailed over Israel, that the Israelites should place their children in the building, so that a man placed his son in the wall and put mortar over him, while his eyes wept over him, and his tears ran down upon his child.

(Jasher 77:19)
And the task-masters of Egypt did so to the babes of Israel for many days, and no one pitied or had compassion over the babes of the children of Israel.

(Jasher 77:20)
And the number of all the children killed in the building was two hundred and seventy, some whom they had built upon instead of the bricks which had been left deficient by their fathers, and some whom they had drawn out dead from the building.

(Jasher 77:21)
And the labor imposed upon the children of Israel in the days of Adikam exceeded in hardship that which they performed in the days of his father.

(...Exodus 2:23) (Jasher 77:22)
    And the children of Israel sighed every day by reason of the bondage, and they cried for they had said to themselves, Behold when Pharaoh shall die, his son will rise up and lighten our work!

(Jasher 77:23)
    But they increased the latter work more than the former, and the children of Israel sighed at this and their cry ascended to God on account of their labor.

(...Exodus 2:23)
    And their cry came up to God by reason of the bondage.

(Exodus 2:24) (Jasher 77:24)
    And God heard the voice of the children of Israel and their groaning, and God remembered to them his covenant which he had made with Abraham, with Isaac, and with Jacob.

(Jasher 77:25)
    And God saw the burden of the children of Israel, and their heavy work in those days, and he determined to deliver them.

(Exodus 2:25)
    And God looked upon the children of Israel, and God had respect to them.

(Jasher 78:11)
    And Pharaoh king of Egypt greatly increased the labor of the children of Israel in those days, and continued to make his yoke heavier upon the children of Israel.

(Jasher 78:12)
    And he ordered a proclamation to be made in Egypt, saying,

Give no more straw to the people to make bricks with, let them go and gather themselves straw as they can find it.

(Jasher 78:13)
Also the tale of bricks which they shall make let them give each day, and diminish nothing from them, for they are idle in their work.

(Jasher 78:14)
And the children of Israel heard this, and they mourned and sighed, and they cried to the Lord on account of the bitterness of their souls.

(Jasher 78:15)
And the Lord heard the cries of the children of Israel, and saw the oppression with which the Egyptians oppressed them.

(Jasher 78:16)
And the Lord was jealous of his people and his inheritance, and heard their voice, and he resolved to take them out of the affliction of Egypt, to give them the land of Canaan for a possession.

The History of Ancient Israel

Exodus: Chapter Three

(Exodus 3:1...) (Jasher 79:1)
  Now in those days Moses kept the flock of Jethro / Reuel the Midianite his father in law, the priest of Midian: and he led the flock to the backside of the desert, beyond the wilderness of Sin, and the stick which he took from his father-in-law was in his hand.

(...Exodus 3:1) (Jasher 79:2)
  And it came to pass one day that a kid of goats strayed from the flock, and Moses pursued it and came to the mountain of God, even to Horeb.

(Exodus 3:2) (Jasher 79:3)
  And when he came to Horeb, the angel of the LORD appeared to him in a flame of fire out of the midst of a bush: and he looked, and, behold, he found the bush burned with fire, and the bush was not consumed.

(Exodus 3:3) (Jasher 79:4...)
  And Moses was greatly astonished at this sight and said, I will now turn aside, and he approached to see this great sight, why the bush is not burnt.

(Exodus 3:4) (...Jasher 79:4...)
  And when the LORD saw that he turned aside to see, God called to him out of the fire in the midst of the bush, and said, Moses, Moses. And he said, Here am I.

(Exodus 3:5)
> And he said, Draw not nigh hither: put off your shoes from off your feet, for the place where you stand is holy ground.

(Exodus 3:6)
> Moreover he said, I am the God of your father, the God of Abraham, the God of Isaac, and the God of Jacob. And Moses hid his face; for he was afraid to look upon God.

(Exodus 3:7)
> And the LORD said, I have surely seen the affliction of my people which are in Egypt, and have heard their cry by reason of their taskmasters; for I know their sorrows;

(Exodus 3:8)
> And I am come down to deliver them out of the hand of the Egyptians, and to bring them up out of that land to a good land and a large, to a land flowing with milk and honey; to the place of the Canaanites, and the Hittites, and the Amorites, and the Perizzites, and the Hivites, and the Jebusites.

(Exodus 3:9)
> Now therefore, behold, the cry of the children of Israel is come to me: and I have also seen the oppression wherewith the Egyptians oppress them.

(Exodus 3:10)
> Come now therefore, and I will send you to Pharaoh, that you may bring forth my people the children of Israel out of Egypt.

(...Jasher 79:4)
> And the Lord commanded him to go down to Egypt, to Pharaoh king of Egypt, to send the children of Israel from his service.

(Jasher 79:5)
And the Lord said to Moses, Go, return to Egypt, for all those men who sought your life are dead, and you shall speak to Pharaoh to send forth the children of Israel from his land.

(Exodus 3:11)
And Moses said to God, Who am I, that I should go to Pharaoh, and that I should bring forth the children of Israel out of Egypt?

(Exodus 3:12)
And he said, Certainly I will be with you; and this shall be a token to you, that I have sent you: When you have brought forth the people out of Egypt, you shall serve God upon this mountain.

(Exodus 3:13)
And Moses said to God, Behold, when I come to the children of Israel, and shall say to them, The God of your fathers has sent me to you; and they shall say to me, What is his name? What shall I say to them?

(Exodus 3:14)
And God said to Moses, I AM THAT I AM: and he said, Thus shall you say to the children of Israel, I AM has sent me to you.

(Exodus 3:15)
And God said moreover to Moses, Thus shall you say to the children of Israel, The LORD God of your fathers, the God of Abraham, the God of Isaac, and the God of Jacob, has sent me to you: this is my name forever, and this is my memorial to all generations.

(Exodus 3:16)
> Go, and gather the elders of Israel together, and say to them, The LORD God of your fathers, the God of Abraham, of Isaac, and of Jacob, appeared to me, saying, I have surely visited you, and seen that which is done to you in Egypt:

(Exodus 3:17)
> And I have said, I will bring you up out of the affliction of Egypt to the land of the Canaanites, and the Hittites, and the Amorites, and the Perizzites, and the Hivites, and the Jebusites, to a land flowing with milk and honey.

(Exodus 3:18)
> And they shall hearken to your voice: and you shall come, you and the elders of Israel, to the king of Egypt, and you shall say to him, The LORD God of the Hebrews has met with us: and now let us go, we beseech you, three days' journey into the wilderness, that we may sacrifice to the LORD our God.

(Exodus 3:19)
> And I am sure that the king of Egypt will not let you go, no, not by a mighty hand.

(Exodus 3:20)
> And I will stretch out my hand, and smite Egypt with all my wonders which I will do in the midst thereof: and after that he will let you go.

(Exodus 3:21)
> And I will give this people favor in the sight of the Egyptians: and it shall come to pass, that, when you go, you shall not go empty:

(Exodus 3:22)
But every woman shall borrow of her neighbor, and of her that sojourns in her house, jewels of silver, and jewels of gold, and raiment: and you shall put them upon your sons, and upon your daughters; and you shall spoil the Egyptians.

The History of Ancient Israel

Exodus: Chapter Four

(Exodus 4:1)
>And Moses answered and said, But, behold, they will not believe me, nor hearken to my voice: for they will say, The LORD has not appeared to you.

(Jasher 9:6)
And the Lord showed him to do signs and wonders in Egypt before the eyes of Pharaoh and the eyes of his subjects, in order that they might believe that the Lord had sent him.

(Exodus 4:2)
>And the LORD said to him, What is that in your hand? And he said, A rod.

(Exodus 4:3)
>And he said, Cast it on the ground. And he cast it on the ground, and it became a serpent; and Moses fled from before it.

(Exodus 4:4)
>And the LORD said to Moses, Put forth your hand, and take it by the tail. And he put forth his hand, and caught it, and it became a rod in his hand:

(Exodus 4:5)
>That they may believe that the LORD God of their fathers, the

God of Abraham, the God of Isaac, and the God of Jacob, has appeared to you.

(Exodus 4:6)
And the LORD said furthermore to him, Put now your hand into your bosom. And he put his hand into his bosom: and when he took it out, behold, his hand was leprous as snow.

(Exodus 4:7)
And he said, Put your hand into your bosom again. And he put his hand into his bosom again; and plucked it out of his bosom, and, behold, it was turned again as his other flesh.

(Exodus 4:8)
And it shall come to pass, if they will not believe you, neither hearken to the voice of the first sign, that they will believe the voice of the latter sign.

(Exodus 4:9)
And it shall come to pass, if they will not believe also these two signs, neither hearken to your voice, that you shall take of the water of the river, and pour it upon the dry land: and the water which you take out of the river shall become blood upon the dry land.

(Exodus 4:10)
And Moses said to the LORD, O my Lord, I am not eloquent, neither heretofore, nor since you have spoken to your servant: but I am slow of speech, and of a slow tongue.

(Exodus 4:11)
And the LORD said to him, Who has made man's mouth? Or who makes the dumb, or deaf, or the seeing, or the blind? Have not I the LORD?

Book Six: From Goshen to Sinai

(Exodus 4:12)
> Now therefore go, and I will be with your mouth, and teach you what you shall say.

(Exodus 4:13)
> And he said, O my Lord, send, I pray you, by the hand of him whom you will send.

(Exodus 4:14)
> And the anger of the LORD was kindled against Moses, and he said, Is not Aaron the Levite your brother? I know that he can speak well. And also, behold, he comes forth to meet you: and when he sees you, he will be glad in his heart.

(Exodus 4:15)
> And you shall speak to him, and put words in his mouth: and I will be with your mouth, and with his mouth, and will teach you what you shall do.

(Exodus 4:16)
> And he shall be your spokesman to the people: and he shall be, even he shall be to you instead of a mouth, and you shall be to him instead of God.

(Exodus 4:17)
> And you shall take this rod in your hand, wherewith you shall do signs.

(Exodus 4:18) (Jasher 79:7)
> And Moses hearkened to all that the Lord had commanded him, and he went and returned to Jethro his father in law and told him the thing, and said to him, Let me go, I pray you, and return to my brethren which are in Egypt, and see whether they be yet alive. And Jethro / Reuel said to Moses, Go in peace.

(Exodus 4:19)
>And the LORD said to Moses in Midian, Go, return into Egypt: for all the men are dead which sought your life.

(Exodus 4:20) (Jasher 79:8...)
>And Moses rose up to go to Egypt, and he took his wife and his sons with him, and set them upon a donkey, and he returned to the land of Egypt: and Moses took the rod of God in his hand.

(Jubilees 48:1...)
>And Moses returned into Egypt in the second week in the second year in the fiftieth jubilee.

(Exodus 4:21)
>And the LORD said to Moses, When you go to return into Egypt, see that you do all those wonders before Pharaoh, which I have put in your hand: but I will harden his heart, that he shall not let the people go.

(Exodus 4:22)
>And you shall say to Pharaoh, Thus says the LORD, Israel is my son, even my firstborn:

(Exodus 4:23)
>And I say to you, Let my son go, that he may serve me: and if you refuse to let him go, behold, I will slay your son, even your firstborn.

(Jubilees 48:2)
>And Moses knew what He spoke to him on Mount Sinai, and what prince Mastêmâ desired to do with him when he was returning into Egypt on the way when he met him at the lodging-place.

Book Six: From Goshen to Sinai

(Jubilees 48:3)
Did he not with all his power seek to slay Moses and deliver the Egyptians out of his hand when he saw that he was sent to execute judgment and vengeance on the Egyptians?

(Jubilees 48:4...)
And God delivered him out of his hand.

(Exodus 4:24) (...Jasher 79:8)
And it came to pass by the way he was in the inn in the road, that an angel of the LORD God met him, and sought an occasion against him to kill him.

(Jasher 79:9)
And he wished to kill him on account of his first born son, because he had not circumcised him, and had transgressed the covenant which the Lord had made with Abraham.

(Jasher 79:10)
For Moses had hearkened to the words of his father-in-law which he had spoken to him, not to circumcise his first born son, therefore he circumcised him not.

(Jasher 79:11)
And Zipporah saw the angel of the Lord seeking an occasion against Moses, and she knew that this thing was owing to his not having circumcised her son Gershom.

(Exodus 4:25) (Jasher 79:12...)
Then Zipporah hastened and took a sharp rock stone that was there, and cut off the foreskin of her son, and cast it at his feet, and said, Surely a bloody husband are you to me.

(Exodus 4:26)
So he let him go: then she said, A bloody husband you are, because of the circumcision.

(...Jasher 79:12)
And Zipporah delivered her husband and her son from the hand of the angel of the Lord.

(Jasher 79:13)
And Aaron the son of Amram, the brother of Moses, was in Egypt walking at the river side on that day.

(Exodus 4:27) (Jasher 79:14)
And the LORD appeared to him in that place, and he said to Aaron, Go into the wilderness to meet Moses. And he went, and met him in the mount of God, and kissed him.

(Exodus 4:28)
And Moses told Aaron all the words of the LORD who had sent him, and all the signs which he had commanded him.

(Jasher 79:15)
And Aaron lifted up his eyes, and saw Zipporah the wife of Moses and her children, and he said to Moses, Who are these to you?

(Jasher 79:16)
And Moses said to him, They are my wife and sons, which God gave to me in Midian; and the thing grieved Aaron on account of the woman and her children.

(Jasher 79:17)
And Aaron said to Moses, Send away the woman and her

children that they may go to her father's house, and Moses hearkened to the words of Aaron, and did so.

(Jasher 79:18)
And Zipporah returned with her children, and they went to the house of Reuel, and remained there until the time arrived when the Lord had visited his people, and brought them forth from Egypt from the hand at Pharaoh.

(Exodus 4:29) (Jasher 79:18...)
And Moses and Aaron went to Egypt to the community of the children of Israel, and gathered together all the elders of the children of Israel:

(Exodus 4:30) (...Jasher 79:18...)
And Aaron spoke all the words which the LORD had spoken to Moses, and did the signs in the sight of the people.

(Exodus 4:31) (...Jasher 79:18)
And the people believed and rejoiced an exceeding great rejoicing when they heard that the LORD had visited the children of Israel, and that he had looked upon their affliction, then they bowed their heads and worshipped.

(Jasher 79:20)
And Moses and Aaron rose up early on the next day, and they went to the house of Pharaoh, and they took in their hands the stick of God.

Exodus: Chapter Five

(Jasher 79:21)
And when they came to the king's gate, two young lions were confined there with iron instruments, and no person went out or came in from before them, unless those whom the king ordered to come, when the conjurers came and withdrew the lions by their incantations, and this brought them to the king.

(Jasher 79:22)
And Moses hastened and lifted up the stick upon the lions, and he loosed them, and Moses and Aaron came into the king's house.

(Jasher 79:23)
The lions also came with them in joy, and they followed them and rejoiced as a dog rejoices over his master when he comes from the field.

(Exodus 5:1...) (Jasher 79:24)
And afterward Moses and Aaron went in. And when Pharaoh saw this thing he was astonished at it, and he was greatly terrified at the report, for their appearance was like the appearance of the children of God.

(...Exodus 5:1) (Jasher 79:25)
And Pharaoh said to Moses, What do you require? And they answered him, and told Pharaoh, The Lord God of the Hebrews has sent us to you, to say, Thus says the LORD God

of Israel, Let my people go, that they may hold a feast to me in the wilderness. Send forth my people that they may serve me.

(Jasher 79:26)
And when Pharaoh heard their words he was greatly terrified before them, and he said to them, Go today and come back to me tomorrow, and they did according to the word of the king.

(Jasher 79:27)
And when they had gone Pharaoh sent for Balaam the magician and to Jannes and Jambres his sons, and to all the magicians and conjurers and counselors which belonged to the king, and they all came and sat before the king.

(Jasher 79:28)
And the king told them all the words which Moses and his brother Aaron had spoken to him, and the magicians said to the king, But how came the men to you, on account of the lions which were confined at the gate?

(Jasher 79:29)
And the king said, Because they lifted up their rod against the lions and loosed them, and came to me, and the lions also rejoiced at them as a dog rejoices to meet his master.

(Jasher 79:30)
And Balaam the son of Beor the magician answered the king, saying, These are none else than magicians like ourselves.

(Jasher 79:31)
Now therefore send for them, and let them come and we will try them, and the king did so.

Book Six: From Goshen to Sinai

(Jasher 79:32)
And in the morning Pharaoh sent for Moses and Aaron to come before the king, and they took the rod of God, and came to the king and spoke to him, saying,

(Jasher 79:33)
Thus said the Lord God of the Hebrews, Send my people that they may serve me.

(Exodus 5:2)
And Pharaoh said, Who is the LORD, that I should obey his voice to let Israel go? I know not the LORD, neither will I let Israel go.

(Exodus 5:3)
And they said, The God of the Hebrews has met with us: let us go, we pray you, three days' journey into the desert, and sacrifice to the LORD our God; lest he fall upon us with pestilence, or with the sword.

(Exodus 5:4)
And the king of Egypt said to them, Why do you, Moses and Aaron, let the people from their works? Get you to your burdens.

(Exodus 5:5)
And Pharaoh said, Behold, the people of the land now are many, and you make them rest from their burdens.

(Exodus 5:6)
And Pharaoh commanded the same day the taskmasters of the people, and their officers, saying,

(Exodus 5:7)
> You shall no more give the people straw to make brick, as heretofore: let them go and gather straw for themselves.

(Exodus 5:8)
> And the tale of the bricks, which they did make heretofore, you shall lay upon them; you shall not diminish ought thereof: for they be idle; therefore they cry, saying, Let us go and sacrifice to our God.

(Exodus 5:9)
> Let there more work be laid upon the men, that they may labor therein; and let them not regard vain words.

(Exodus 5:10)
> And the taskmasters of the people went out, and their officers, and they spoke to the people, saying, Thus says Pharaoh, I will not give you straw.

(Exodus 5:11)
> Go you, get you straw where you can find it: yet not ought of your work shall be diminished.

(Exodus 5:12)
> So the people were scattered abroad throughout all the land of Egypt to gather stubble instead of straw.

(Exodus 5:13)
> And the taskmasters hasted them, saying, Fulfill your works, your daily tasks, as when there was straw.

(Exodus 5:14)
> And the officers of the children of Israel, which Pharaoh's taskmasters had set over them, were beaten, and demanded,

Book Six: From Goshen to Sinai

Why have you not fulfilled your task in making brick both yesterday and today, as heretofore?

(Exodus 5:15)
Then the officers of the children of Israel came and cried to Pharaoh, saying, Why do you deal thus with your servants?

(Exodus 5:16)
There is no straw given to your servants, and they say to us, Make brick: and, behold, your servants are beaten; but the fault is in your own people.

(Exodus 5:17)
But he said, You are idle, you are idle: therefore you say, Let us go and do sacrifice to the LORD.

(Exodus 5:18)
Go therefore now, and work; for there shall no straw be given you, yet shall you deliver the tale of bricks.

(Exodus 5:19)
And the officers of the children of Israel did see that they were in evil case, after it was said, You shall not diminish from your bricks of your daily task.

(Exodus 5:20)
And they met Moses and Aaron, who stood in the way, as they came forth from Pharaoh:

(Exodus 5:21)
And they said to them, The LORD looks upon you, and judges; because you have made our savor to be abhorred in the eyes of Pharaoh, and in the eyes of his servants, to put a sword in their hand to slay us.

(Exodus 5:22)
And Moses returned to the LORD, and said, Lord, why have you so evil entreated this people? Why is it that you have sent me?

(Exodus 5:23)
For since I came to Pharaoh to speak in your name, he has done evil to this people; neither have you delivered your people at all.

Exodus: Chapter Six

(Exodus 6:1)
> Then the LORD said to Moses, Now shall you see what I will do to Pharaoh: for with a strong hand shall he let them go, and with a strong hand shall he drive them out of his land.

(Exodus 6:2)
> And God spoke to Moses, and said to him, I am the LORD:

(Exodus 6:3)
> And I appeared to Abraham, to Isaac, and to Jacob, by the name of God Almighty, but by my name JEHOVAH was I not known to them.

(Exodus 6:4)
> And I have also established my covenant with them, to give them the land of Canaan, the land of their pilgrimage, wherein they were strangers.

(Exodus 6:5)
> And I have also heard the groaning of the children of Israel, whom the Egyptians keep in bondage; and I have remembered my covenant.

(Exodus 6:6)
> Why say to the children of Israel, I am the LORD, and I will bring you out from under the burdens of the Egyptians, and I will rid you out of their bondage, and I will redeem you with

an outstretched arm, and with great judgments:

(Exodus 6:7)
And I will take you to me for a people, and I will be to you a God: and you shall know that I am the LORD your God, which brings you out from under the burdens of the Egyptians.

(Exodus 6:8)
And I will bring you in to the land, concerning the which I did swear to give it to Abraham, to Isaac, and to Jacob; and I will give it you for a heritage: I am the LORD.

(Exodus 6:9)
And Moses spoke so to the children of Israel: but they hearkened not to Moses for anguish of spirit, and for cruel bondage.

(Exodus 6:10)
And the LORD spoke to Moses, saying,

(Exodus 6:11)
Go in, speak to Pharaoh king of Egypt, that he let the children of Israel go out of his land.

(Exodus 6:12)
And Moses spoke before the LORD, saying, Behold, the children of Israel have not hearkened to me; how then shall Pharaoh hear me, who am of uncircumcised lips?

(Exodus 6:13)
And the LORD spoke to Moses and to Aaron, and gave them a charge to the children of Israel, and to Pharaoh king of Egypt, to bring the children of Israel out of the land of Egypt.

Book Six: From Goshen to Sinai

(Exodus 6:14)
These be the heads of their fathers' houses: The sons of Reuben the firstborn of Israel; Hanoch, and Pallu, Hezron, and Carmi: these be the families of Reuben.

(Exodus 6:15)
And the sons of Simeon; Jemuel, and Jamin, and Ohad, and Jachin, and Zohar, and Shaul the son of a Canaanite woman: these are the families of Simeon.

(Exodus 6:16)
And these are the names of the sons of Levi according to their generations; Gershon, and Kohath, and Merari: and the years of the life of Levi were a hundred thirty and seven years.

(Exodus 6:17)
The sons of Gershon; Libni, and Shimi, according to their families.

(Exodus 6:18)
And the sons of Kohath; Amram, and Izhar, and Hebron, and Uzziel: and the years of the life of Kohath were an hundred thirty and three years.

(Exodus 6:19)
And the sons of Merari; Mahali and Mushi: these are the families of Levi according to their generations.

(Exodus 6:20)
And Amram took him Jochebed his father's sister to wife; and she bare him Aaron and Moses: and the years of the life of Amram were an hundred and thirty and seven years.

(Exodus 6:21)
And the sons of Izhar; Korah, and Nepheg, and Zichri.

(Exodus 6:22)
And the sons of Uzziel; Mishael, and Elzaphan, and Zithri.

(Exodus 6:23)
And Aaron took him Elisheba, daughter of Amminadab, sister of Naashon, to wife; and she bare him Nadab, and Abihu, Eleazar, and Ithamar.

(Exodus 6:24)
And the sons of Korah; Assir, and Elkanah, and Abiasaph: these are the families of the Korhites.

(Exodus 6:25)
And Eleazar Aaron's son took him one of the daughters of Putiel to wife; and she bare him Phinehas: these are the heads of the fathers of the Levites according to their families.

(Exodus 6:26)
These are that Aaron and Moses, to whom the LORD said, Bring out the children of Israel from the land of Egypt according to their armies.

(Exodus 6:27)
These are they which spoke to Pharaoh king of Egypt, to bring out the children of Israel from Egypt: these are that Moses and Aaron.

(Exodus 6:28)
And it came to pass on the day when the LORD spoke to Moses in the land of Egypt,

Book Six: From Goshen to Sinai

(Exodus 6:29)
That the LORD spoke to Moses, saying, I am the LORD: speak you to Pharaoh king of Egypt all that I say to you.

(Exodus 6:30)
And Moses said before the LORD, Behold, I am of uncircumcised lips, and how shall Pharaoh hearken to me?

The History of Ancient Israel

Exodus: Chapter Seven

(Exodus 7:1)
> And the LORD said to Moses, See, I have made you a god to Pharaoh: and Aaron your brother shall be your prophet.

(Exodus 7:2)
> You shall speak all that I command you: and Aaron your brother shall speak to Pharaoh, that he send the children of Israel out of his land.

(Exodus 7:3)
> And I will harden Pharaoh's heart, and multiply my signs and my wonders in the land of Egypt.

(Exodus 7:4)
> But Pharaoh shall not hearken to you, that I may lay my hand upon Egypt, and bring forth mine armies, and my people the children of Israel, out of the land of Egypt by great judgments.

(Exodus 7:5)
> And the Egyptians shall know that I am the LORD, when I stretch forth mine hand upon Egypt, and bring out the children of Israel from among them.

(Exodus 7:6)
> And Moses and Aaron did as the LORD commanded them, so did they.

(Exodus 7:7)
And Moses was fourscore years old, and Aaron fourscore and three years old, when they spoke to Pharaoh.

(Exodus 7:8)
And the LORD spoke to Moses and to Aaron, saying,

(Exodus 7:9)
When Pharaoh shall speak to you, saying, Show a miracle for you: then you shall say to Aaron, Take your rod, and cast it before Pharaoh, and it shall become a serpent.

(Exodus 7:10...)
And Moses and Aaron went in to Pharaoh, and they did so as the LORD had commanded:

(Jasher 79:34)
And the king said to them, But who will believe you that you are the messengers of God and that you come to me by his order?

(Jasher 79:35)
Now therefore give a wonder or sign in this matter, and then the words which you speak will be believed.

(...Exodus 7:10) (Jasher 79:36)
And Aaron hastened cast down his rod out of his hand before Pharaoh, and before his servants, and it became a serpent.

(Exodus 7:11) (Jasher 79:37...)
Then Pharaoh also called the wise men and the sorcerers: now the magicians of Egypt, and the sorcerers saw this and they also did in like manner with their enchantments.

Book Six: From Goshen to Sinai

(Exodus 7:12) (...Jasher 79:37)
For they cast down every man his rod upon the ground, and they became serpents: and the serpent of Aaron's rod lifted up its head and opened its mouth to swallow the rods of the magicians.

(Jasher 79:39)
And Balaam the magician answered and said, This thing has been from the days of old, that a serpent should swallow its fellow, and that living things devour each other.

(Jasher 79:40)
Now therefore restore it to a rod as it was at first, and we will also restore our rods as they were at first, and if your rod shall swallow our rods, then shall we know that the spirit of God is in you, and if not, you are only an artificer like to ourselves.

(Jasher 79:41)
And Aaron hastened and stretched forth his hand and caught hold of the serpent's tail and it became a rod in his hand, and the sorcerers did the like with their rods, and they got hold, each man of the tail of his serpent, and they became rods as at first.

(Exodus 7:12) (Jasher 79:42)
And when they were restored to rods, Aaron's rod swallowed up their rods.

(Jasher 79:43)
And when the king saw this thing, he ordered the book of records that related to the kings of Egypt, to be brought, and they brought the book of records, the chronicles of the kings of Egypt, in which all the idols of Egypt were inscribed, for they thought of finding therein the name of Jehovah, but they found it not.

(Jasher 79:44)
And Pharaoh said to Moses and Aaron, Behold I have not found the name of your God written in this book, and his name I know not.

(Jasher 79:45)
And the counselors and wise men answered the king, We have heard that the God of the Hebrews is a son of the wise, the son of ancient kings.

(Jasher 79:46)
And Pharaoh turned to Moses and Aaron and said to them, I know not the Lord whom you have declared, neither will I send his people.

(Jasher 79:47)
And they answered and said to the king, The Lord God of Gods is his name, and he proclaimed his name over us from the days of our ancestors, and sent us, saying, Go to Pharaoh and say to him, Send my people that they may serve me.

(Jasher 79:48)
Now therefore send us, that we may take a journey for three days in the wilderness, and there may sacrifice to him, for from the days of our going down to Egypt, he has not taken from our hands either burnt offering, oblation or sacrifice, and if you will not send us, his anger will be kindled against you, and he will smite Egypt either with the plague or with the sword.

(Jasher 79:49)
And Pharaoh said to them, Tell me now his power and his might; and they said to him, He created the heaven and the earth, the seas and all their fishes, he formed the light, created

the darkness, caused rain upon the earth and watered it, and made the herbage and grass to sprout, he created man and beast and the animals of the forest, the birds of the air and the fish of the sea, and by his mouth they live and die.

(Jasher 79:50)
Surely he created you in your mother's womb, and put into you the breath of life, and reared you and placed you upon the royal throne of Egypt, and he will take your breath and soul from you, and return to the ground from where you were taken.

(Jasher 79:51)
And the anger of the king was kindled at their words, and he said to them, But who among all the Gods of nations can do this? My river is my own, and I have made it for myself.

(Exodus 7:13)
And God hardened Pharaoh's heart, that he hearkened not to them; as the LORD had said.

(Jasher 79:52)
And he drove them from him, and he ordered the labor upon Israel to be more severe than it was yesterday and before.

(Jasher 79:53)
And Moses and Aaron went out from the king's presence, and they saw the children of Israel in an evil condition for the task-masters had made their labor exceedingly heavy.

(Jasher 79:54)
And Moses returned to the Lord and said, Why have you ill treated your people? For since I came to speak to Pharaoh what you did send me for, he has exceedingly ill used the children of Israel.

(Jasher 79:55)
And the Lord said to Moses, Behold you will see that with an outstretched hand and heavy plagues, Pharaoh will send the children of Israel from his land.

(Jasher 79:56)
And Moses and Aaron dwelt among their brothers the children of Israel in Egypt.

(Jasher 79:57)
And as for the children of Israel the Egyptians embittered their lives, with the heavy work which they imposed upon them.

~ ~ ~

(Jasher 80:1)
And at the end of two years, the Lord again sent Moses to Pharaoh to bring forth the children of Israel, and to send them out of the land of Egypt.

(Jasher 80:2)
And Moses went and came to the house of Pharaoh, and he spoke to him the words of the Lord who had sent him, but Pharaoh would not hearken to the voice of the Lord, and God roused his might in Egypt upon Pharaoh and his subjects, and God smote Pharaoh and his people with very great and sore plagues.

(Exodus 7:14)
And the LORD said to Moses, Pharaoh's heart is hardened, he refuses to let the people go.

(Exodus 7:15)
> Get you to Pharaoh in the morning; lo, he goes out to the water; and you shall stand by the river's brink against he come; and the rod which was turned to a serpent shall you take in your hand.

(Exodus 7:16)
> And you shall say to him, The LORD God of the Hebrews has sent me to you, saying, Let my people go, that they may serve me in the wilderness: and, behold, hitherto you would not hear.

(Exodus 7:17)
> Thus says the LORD, In this you shall know that I am the LORD: behold, I will smite with the rod that is in mine hand upon the waters which are in the river, and they shall be turned to blood.

(Exodus 7:18)
> And the fish that is in the river shall die, and the river shall stink; and the Egyptians shall loathe to drink of the water of the river.

(Exodus 7:19)
> And the LORD spoke to Moses, Say to Aaron, Take your rod, and stretch out your hand upon the waters of Egypt, upon their streams, upon their rivers, and upon their ponds, and upon all their pools of water, that they may become blood; and that there may be blood throughout all the land of Egypt, both in vessels of wood, and in vessels of stone.

(Exodus 7:20) (Jasher 80:3)
> And Moses and Aaron did so, as the LORD commanded. And the Lord sent by the hand of Aaron and he lifted up the rod,

and smote the waters that were in the river, in the sight of Pharaoh, and in the sight of his servants; and all the waters that were in the river, with all their streams and rivers were turned to blood.

(Exodus 7:21)
And the fish that was in the river died; and the river stank, and the Egyptians could not drink of the water of the river; and there was blood throughout all the land of Egypt.

(Exodus 7:22)
And the magicians of Egypt did so with their enchantments: and Pharaoh's heart was hardened, neither did he hearken to them; as the LORD had said.

(Exodus 7:23)
And Pharaoh turned and went into his house, neither did he set his heart to this also.

(Jasher 80:4)
And when an Egyptian came to drink and draw water, he looked into his pitcher, and behold all the water was turned into blood; and when he came to drink from his cup the water in the cup became blood.

(Jasher 80:5)
And when a woman kneaded her dough and cooked her victuals, their appearance was turned to that of blood.

(Exodus 7:24)
And all the Egyptians dug round about the river for water to drink; for they could not drink of the water of the river.

(Exodus 7:25)
And seven days were fulfilled, after that the LORD had smitten the river.

Exodus: Chapter Eight

(Exodus 8:1)
>And the LORD spoke to Moses, Go to Pharaoh, and say to him, Thus says the LORD, Let my people go, that they may serve me.

(Exodus 8:2)
>And if you refuse to let them go, behold, I will smite all your borders with frogs:

(Exodus 8:3)
>And the river shall bring forth frogs abundantly, which shall go up and come into your house, and into your bedchamber, and upon your bed, and into the house of your servants, and upon your people, and into your ovens, and into your kneading troughs:

(Exodus 8:4)
>And the frogs shall come up both on you, and upon your people, and upon all your servants.

(Exodus 8:5)
>And the LORD spoke to Moses, Say to Aaron, Stretch forth your hand with your rod over the streams, over the rivers, and over the ponds, and cause frogs to come up upon the land of Egypt.

(Exodus 8:6) (Jasher 80:6)
And Aaron stretched out his hand over the waters of Egypt; and the Lord sent again and caused all their waters to bring forth frogs, and the frogs came up, and covered the land of Egypt, and all the frogs came into the houses of the Egyptians.

(Exodus 8:7)
And the magicians did so with their enchantments, and brought up frogs upon the land of Egypt.

(Jasher 80:7)
And when the Egyptians drank, their bellies were filled with frogs and they danced in their bellies as they dance when in the river.

(Jasher 80:8)
And all their drinking water and cooking water turned to frogs, also when they lay in their beds their perspiration bred frogs.

(Exodus 8:8)
Then Pharaoh called for Moses and Aaron, and said, Entreat the LORD, that he may take away the frogs from me, and from my people; and I will let the people go, that they may do sacrifice to the LORD.

(Exodus 8:9)
And Moses said to Pharaoh, Glory over me: when shall I entreat for you, and for your servants, and for your people, to destroy the frogs from you and your houses, that they may remain in the river only?

(Exodus 8:10)
> And he said, Tomorrow. And he said, May it be according to your word: that you may know that there is none like to the LORD our God.

(Exodus 8:11)
> And the frogs shall depart from you, and from your houses, and from your servants, and from your people; they shall remain in the river only.

(Exodus 8:12)
> And Moses and Aaron went out from Pharaoh: and Moses cried to the LORD because of the frogs which he had brought against Pharaoh.

(Exodus 8:13)
> And the LORD did according to the word of Moses; and the frogs died out of the houses, out of the villages, and out of the fields.

(Exodus 8:14)
> And they gathered them together upon heaps: and the land stank.

(Jasher 80:9...)
> Notwithstanding all this the anger of the Lord did not turn from them.

(Exodus 8:15)
> But when Pharaoh saw that there was respite, he hardened his heart, and hearkened not to them; as the LORD had said.

(Exodus 8:16) (...Jasher 80:9)
And his hand was stretched out against all the Egyptians to smite them with every heavy plague. And the LORD said to Moses, Say to Aaron, Stretch out your rod, and smite the dust of the land, that it may become lice throughout all the land of Egypt.

(Exodus 8:17) (Jasher 80:10, 11)
And they did so; for Aaron stretched out his hand with his rod, and smote the dust of the earth, and the Lord sent and smote their dust and it became lice. The lice were also very numerous in the flesh of man, and in beast, and in all the inhabitants of Egypt, also upon the king and queen the Lord sent the lice, and it grieved Egypt exceedingly on account of the lice; all the dust of the land became lice throughout all the land of Egypt to the height of two cubits upon the earth.

(Exodus 8:18)
And the magicians did so with their enchantments to bring forth lice, but they could not: so there were lice upon man, and upon beast.

(Exodus 8:19) (Jasher 80:12)
Then the magicians said to Pharaoh, This is the finger of God: Notwithstanding this, the anger of the Lord did not turn away, and his hand was still stretched out over Egypt, and Pharaoh's heart was hardened, and he hearkened not to them; as the LORD had said.

(Exodus 8:20)
And the LORD said to Moses, Rise up early in the morning, and stand before Pharaoh; lo, he comes forth to the water; and say to him, Thus says the LORD, Let my people go, that they may serve me.

Book Six: From Goshen to Sinai

(Exodus 8:21)
Else, if you will not let my people go, behold, I will send swarms of flies upon you, and upon your servants, and upon your people, and into your houses: and the houses of the Egyptians shall be full of swarms of flies, and also the ground whereon they are.

(Exodus 8:22)
And I will sever in that day the land of Goshen, in which my people dwell, that no swarms of flies shall be there; to the end you may know that I am the LORD in the midst of the earth.

(Exodus 8:23)
And I will put a division between my people and your people: tomorrow shall this sign be.

(Exodus 8:24)
And the LORD did so; and there came a grievous swarm of flies into the house of Pharaoh, and into his servants' houses, and into all the land of Egypt: the land was corrupted by reason of the swarm of flies.

(Jasher 80:13)
And the Lord sent all kinds of beasts of the field into Egypt, and they came and destroyed all Egypt, man and beast, and trees, and all things that were in Egypt.

(Jasher 80:14)
And the Lord sent fiery serpents, scorpions, mice, weasels, toads, together with others creeping in dust.

(Jasher 80:15)
Flies, hornets, fleas, bugs and gnats, each swarm according to its kind.

(Jasher 80:16)
And all reptiles and winged animals according to their kind came to Egypt and grieved the Egyptians exceedingly.

(Jasher 80:17)
And the fleas and flies came into the eyes and ears of the Egyptians.

(Jasher 80:18)
And the hornet came upon them and drove them away, and they removed from it into their inner rooms, and it pursued them.

(Jasher 80:19)
And when the Egyptians hid themselves on account of the swarm of animals, they locked their doors after them, and God ordered the Sulanuth which was in the sea, to come up and go into Egypt.

(Jasher 80:20)
And she had long arms, ten cubits in length of the cubit of a man.

(Jasher 80:21)
And she went upon the roofs and uncovered the rafters and flooring and cut them, and stretched forth her arm into the house and removed the lock and the bolt, and opened the houses of Egypt.

(Jasher 80:22)
Afterward came the swarm of animals into the houses of Egypt, and the swarm of animals destroyed the Egyptians, and it grieved them exceedingly.

Book Six: From Goshen to Sinai

(Exodus 8:25)
And Pharaoh called for Moses and for Aaron, and said, Go you, sacrifice to your God in the land.

(Exodus 8:26)
And Moses said, It is not meet so to do; for we shall sacrifice the abomination of the Egyptians to the LORD our God: lo, shall we sacrifice the abomination of the Egyptians before their eyes, and will they not stone us?

(Exodus 8:27)
We will go three days' journey into the wilderness, and sacrifice to the LORD our God, as he shall command us.

(Exodus 8:28)
And Pharaoh said, I will let you go, that you may sacrifice to the LORD your God in the wilderness; only you shall not go very far away: entreat for me.

(Exodus 8:29)
And Moses said, Behold, I go out from you, and I will entreat the LORD that the swarms of flies may depart from Pharaoh, from his servants, and from his people, tomorrow: but let not Pharaoh deal deceitfully any more in not letting the people go to sacrifice to the LORD.

(Exodus 8:30)
And Moses went out from Pharaoh, and entreated the LORD.

(Exodus 8:31)
And the LORD did according to the word of Moses; and he removed the swarms of flies from Pharaoh, from his servants, and from his people; there remained not one.

(Jasher 80:23)
Notwithstanding this the anger of the Lord did not turn away from the Egyptians, and his hand was yet stretched forth against them.

(Exodus 8:32)
And Pharaoh hardened his heart at this time also, neither would he let the people go.

Exodus: Chapter Nine

(Exodus 9:1)
Then the LORD said to Moses, Go in to Pharaoh, and tell him, Thus says the LORD God of the Hebrews, Let my people go, that they may serve me.

(Exodus 9:2)
For if you refuse to let them go, and will hold them still,

(Exodus 9:3)
Behold, the hand of the LORD is upon your cattle which is in the field, upon the horses, upon the donkeys, upon the camels, upon the oxen, and upon the sheep: there shall be a very grievous murrain.

(Exodus 9:4)
And the LORD shall sever between the cattle of Israel and the cattle of Egypt: and there shall nothing die of all that is the children's of Israel.

(Exodus 9:5)
And the LORD appointed a set time, saying, Tomorrow the LORD shall do this thing in the land.

(Exodus 9:6...) (Jasher 80:24)
And the LORD did that thing on the morrow. And God sent the pestilence, and the pestilence pervaded Egypt, in the

horses and donkeys, and in the camels, in herds of oxen and sheep and in man, and all the cattle of Egypt died:

(Jasher 80:25)
And when the Egyptians rose up early in the morning to take their cattle to pasture they found all their cattle dead.

(...Exodus 9:6) (Jasher 80:26)
    And there remained of the cattle of the Egyptians only one in ten, but of the cattle of the children of Israel in Goshen not one died.

(Exodus 9:7)
    And Pharaoh sent, and, behold, there was not one of the cattle of the Israelites dead. And the heart of Pharaoh was hardened, and he did not let the people go.

(Exodus 9:8)
    And the LORD said to Moses and to Aaron, Take to you handfuls of ashes of the furnace, and let Moses sprinkle it toward the heaven in the sight of Pharaoh.

(Exodus 9:9)
    And it shall become small dust in all the land of Egypt, and shall be a boil breaking forth with blains upon man, and upon beast, throughout all the land of Egypt.

(Exodus 9:10)
    And they took ashes of the furnace, and stood before Pharaoh; and Moses sprinkled it up toward heaven; and it became a boil breaking forth with blains upon man, and upon beast.

(Jasher 80:27)
And God sent a burning inflammation in the flesh of the Egyptians, which burst their skins, and it became a severe itch in all the Egyptians from the soles of their feet to the crowns of their heads.

(Jasher 80:28)
And many boils were in their flesh, that their flesh wasted away until they became rotten and putrid.

(Exodus 9:11)
And the magicians could not stand before Moses because of the boils; for the boil was upon the magicians, and upon all the Egyptians.

(Jasher 80:29)
Notwithstanding this the anger of the Lord did not turn away, and his hand was still stretched out over all Egypt.

(Exodus 9:12)
And the LORD hardened the heart of Pharaoh, and he hearkened not to them; as the LORD had spoken to Moses.

(Exodus 9:13)
And the LORD said to Moses, Rise up early in the morning, and stand before Pharaoh, and say to him, Thus says the LORD God of the Hebrews, Let my people go, that they may serve me.

(Exodus 9:14)
For I will at this time send all my plagues upon your heart, and upon your servants, and upon your people; that you may know that there is none like me in all the earth.

(Exodus 9:15)
> For now I will stretch out my hand, that I may smite you and your people with pestilence; and you shall be cut off from the earth.

(Exodus 9:16)
> And in very deed for this cause have I raised you up, for to shew in you my power; and that my name may be declared throughout all the earth.

(Exodus 9:17)
> As yet you exalt yourself against my people, that you will not let them go?

(Exodus 9:18)
> Behold, tomorrow about this time I will cause it to rain a very grievous hail, such as has not been in Egypt since the foundation thereof even until now.

(Exodus 9:19)
> Send therefore now, and gather your cattle, and all that you have in the field; for upon every man and beast which shall be found in the field, and shall not be brought home, the hail shall come down upon them, and they shall die.

(Exodus 9:20)
> He that feared the word of the LORD among the servants of Pharaoh made his servants and his cattle flee into the houses:

(Exodus 9:21)
> And he that regarded not the word of the LORD left his servants and his cattle in the field.

Book Six: From Goshen to Sinai

(Exodus 9:22)
And the LORD said to Moses, Stretch forth your hand toward heaven, that there may be hail in all the land of Egypt, upon man, and upon beast, and upon every herb of the field, throughout the land of Egypt.

(Exodus 9:23) (Jasher 80:30...)
And Moses stretched forth his rod toward heaven: and the LORD sent thunder and hail, and the fire ran along upon the ground; and the LORD rained hail upon the land of Egypt.

(Exodus 9:24) (...Jasher 80:30..., 31...)
So there was hail, and fire mingled with the hail, very grievous, therefore the hail and the fire consumed all things. Such as there was none like it in all the land of Egypt since it became a nation.

(Exodus 9:25) (...Jasher 80:30, ...31)
And the hail smote throughout all the land of Egypt all that was in the field, both man and beast; and the hail smote their vines, every herb of the field became dry and perished, and it broke every fruit tree of the field, and dried them up that they fell upon them.

(Jasher 80:32)
Also men and beasts that were found abroad perished of the flames of fire and of the hail, and all the young lions were exhausted.

(Exodus 9:26)
Only in the land of Goshen, where the children of Israel were, was there no hail.

(Exodus 9:27)
>And Pharaoh sent, and called for Moses and Aaron, and said to them, I have sinned this time: the LORD is righteous, and I and my people are wicked.

(Exodus 9:28)
>Entreat the LORD (for it is enough) that there no more be mighty thunderings and hail; and I will let you go, and you shall stay no longer.

(Exodus 9:29)
>And Moses said to him, As soon as I am gone out of the city, I will spread abroad my hands to the LORD; and the thunder shall cease, neither shall there be any more hail; that you may know how that the earth is the LORD'S.

(Exodus 9:30)
>But as for you and your servants, I know that you will not yet fear the LORD God.

(Exodus 9:31)
>And the flax and the barley were smitten: for the barley was in the ear, and the flax was bolled.

(Exodus 9:32)
>But the wheat and the rye were not smitten: for they were not grown up.

(Exodus 9:33)
>And Moses went out of the city from Pharaoh, and spread abroad his hands to the LORD: and the thunders and hail ceased, and the rain was not poured upon the earth.

(Exodus 9:34)
And when Pharaoh saw that the rain and the hail and the thunders were ceased, he sinned yet more, and hardened his heart, he and his servants.

(Exodus 9:35)
And the heart of Pharaoh was hardened, neither would he let the children of Israel go; as the LORD had spoken by Moses.

The History of Ancient Israel

Exodus: Chapter Ten

(Exodus 10:1)
>And the LORD said to Moses, Go in to Pharaoh: for I have hardened his heart, and the heart of his servants, that I might show these my signs before him:

(Exodus 10:2)
>And that you may tell in the ears of your son, and of your son's son, what things I have wrought in Egypt, and my signs which I have done among them; that you may know how that I am the LORD.

(Exodus 10:3)
>And Moses and Aaron came in to Pharaoh, and said to him, Thus says the LORD God of the Hebrews, How long will you refuse to humble yourself before me? Let my people go, that they may serve me.

(Exodus 10:4)
>Else, if you refuse to let my people go, behold, tomorrow I will bring the locusts into your coast:

(Exodus 10:5)
>And they shall cover the face of the earth, that one cannot be able to see the earth: and they shall eat the residue of that which is escaped, which remains to you from the hail, and shall eat every tree which grows for you out of the field:

(Exodus 10:6)
> And they shall fill your houses, and the houses of all your servants, and the houses of all the Egyptians; which neither your fathers, nor your fathers' fathers have seen, since the day that they were upon the earth to this day. And he turned himself, and went out from Pharaoh.

(Exodus 10:7)
> And Pharaoh's servants said to him, How long shall this man be a snare to us? Let the men go, that they may serve the LORD their God: know you not yet that Egypt is destroyed?

(Exodus 10:8)
> And Moses and Aaron were brought again to Pharaoh: and he said to them, Go, serve the LORD your God: but who are they that shall go?

(Exodus 10:9)
> And Moses said, We will go with our young and with our old, with our sons and with our daughters, with our flocks and with our herds will we go; for we must hold a feast to the LORD.

(Exodus 10:10)
> And he said to them, Let the LORD be so with you, as I will let you go, and your little ones: look to it; for evil is before you.

(Exodus 10:11)
> Not so: go now you that are men, and serve the LORD; for that you did desire. And they were driven out from Pharaoh's presence.

(Exodus 10:12)
> And the LORD said to Moses, Stretch out your hand over the land of Egypt for the locusts, that they may come up upon the

land of Egypt, and eat every herb of the land, even all that the hail has left.

(Exodus 10:13)
And Moses stretched forth his rod over the land of Egypt, and the LORD brought an east wind upon the land all that day, and all that night; and when it was morning, the east wind brought the locusts.

(Jasher 80:33...)
And the Lord sent and brought numerous locusts into Egypt, the Chasel, Salom, Chargol, and Chagole, locusts each of its kind.

(Exodus 10:14)
And the locusts went up over all the land of Egypt, and rested in all the coasts of Egypt: very grievous were they; before them there were no such locusts as they, neither after them shall be such.

(Exodus 10:15) (...Jasher 80:33)
For they covered the face of the whole earth, so that the land was darkened; and they ate every herb of the land, and all the fruit of the trees, all which the hail had left: and there remained not any green thing in the trees, or in the herbs of the field, through all the land of Egypt.

(Jasher 80:34)
Then the Egyptians rejoiced at the locusts, although they consumed the produce of the field, and they caught them in abundance and salted them for food.

(Exodus 10:16)
Then Pharaoh called for Moses and Aaron in haste; and he

said, I have sinned against the LORD your God, and against you.

(Exodus 10:17)
Now therefore forgive, I pray you, my sin only this once, and entreat the LORD your God, that he may take away from me this death only.

(Exodus 10:18)
And he went out from Pharaoh, and entreated the LORD.

(Exodus 10:19) (Jasher 80:35)
And the LORD turned a mighty strong west wind, which took away all the locusts, even those that were salted, and cast them into the Red sea; there remained not one locust in all the coasts of Egypt.

(Exodus 10:20)
But the LORD hardened Pharaoh's heart, so that he would not let the children of Israel go.

(Exodus 10:21)
And the LORD said to Moses, Stretch out your hand toward heaven, that there may be darkness over the land of Egypt, even darkness which may be felt.

(Exodus 10:22) (Jasher 80:36)
And Moses stretched forth his hand toward heaven; And God sent darkness upon Egypt, and there was a thick darkness in all the land of Egypt and Pathros three days , so that a man could not see his hand when he lifted it to his mouth.

(Jasher 80:37)
At that time died many of the people of Israel who had rebelled

against the Lord and who would not hearken to Moses and Aaron, and believed not in them that God had sent them.

(Jasher 80:38)
And who had said, We will not go forth from Egypt lest we perish with hunger in a desolate wilderness, and who would not hearken to the voice of Moses.

(Jasher 80:39)
And the Lord plagued them in the three days of darkness, and the Israelites buried them in those days, without the Egyptians knowing of them or rejoicing over them.

(Exodus 10:23) (Jasher 80:40)
And the darkness was very great in Egypt, they saw not one another, and any person who was standing when the darkness came, remained standing in his place, and he that was sitting remained sitting, and he that was lying continued lying in the same state, and he that was walking remained sitting upon the ground in the same spot; neither rose any from his place for three days: and this thing happened to all the Egyptians, until the darkness had passed away. But all the children of Israel had light in their dwellings.

(Exodus 10:24)
And Pharaoh called to Moses, and said, Go you, serve the LORD; only let your flocks and your herds be stayed: let your little ones also go with you.

(Exodus 10:25)
And Moses said, You must give us also sacrifices and burnt offerings, that we may sacrifice to the LORD our God.

(Exodus 10:26)
> Our cattle also shall go with us; there shall not a hoof be left behind; for thereof must we take to serve the LORD our God; and we know not with what we must serve the LORD, until we come thither.

(Exodus 10:27)
> But the LORD hardened Pharaoh's heart, and he would not let them go.

(Exodus 10:28)
> And Pharaoh said to him, Get you from me, take heed to yourself, see my face no more; for in that day you see my face you shall die.

(Exodus 10:29)
> And Moses said, You have spoken well, I will see your face again no more.

Exodus: Chapter Eleven

(Exodus 11:1)
And the LORD said to Moses, Yet will I bring one plague more upon Pharaoh, and upon Egypt; afterwards he will let you go hence: when he shall let you go, he shall surely thrust you out hence altogether.

(Jasher 80:41)
And the days of darkness passed away, and the Lord sent Moses and Aaron to the children of Israel,

(Exodus 11:2)
Speak now in the ears of the people, and let every man borrow of his neighbor, and every woman of her neighbor, jewels of silver, and jewels of gold.

(Exodus 11:3)
And the LORD gave the people favor in the sight of the Egyptians. Moreover the man Moses was very great in the land of Egypt, in the sight of Pharaoh's servants, and in the sight of the people.

(Exodus 11:4)
And Moses said, Thus says the LORD, About midnight will I go out into the midst of Egypt:

(Exodus 11:5)
And all the firstborn in the land of Egypt shall die, from the

firstborn of Pharaoh that sits upon his throne, even to the firstborn of the maidservant that is behind the mill; and all the firstborn of beasts.

(Exodus 11:6)
And there shall be a great cry throughout all the land of Egypt, such as there was none like it, nor shall be like it any more.

(Exodus 11:7)
But against any of the children of Israel shall not a dog move his tongue, against man or beast: that you may know how that the LORD doth put a difference between the Egyptians and Israel.

(Exodus 11:8)
And all these your servants shall come down to me, and bow down themselves to me, saying, Get out, and all the people that follow you: and after that I will go out. And he went out from Pharaoh in a great anger.

(Exodus 11:9)
And the LORD said to Moses, Pharaoh shall not hearken to you; that my wonders may be multiplied in the land of Egypt.

(Exodus 11:10)
And Moses and Aaron did all these wonders before Pharaoh: and the LORD hardened Pharaoh's heart, so that he would not let the children of Israel go out of his land.

Exodus: Chapter Twelve

(Exodus 12:1)
And the LORD spoke to Moses and Aaron in the land of Egypt, saying,

(Exodus 12:2)
This month shall be to you the beginning of months: it shall be the first month of the year to you.

(Exodus 12:3)
Speak you to all the congregation of Israel, saying, In the tenth day of this month they shall take to them every man a lamb, according to the house of their fathers, a lamb for a house:

(Exodus 12:4)
And if the household be too little for the lamb, let him and his neighbor next to his house take it according to the number of the souls; every man according to his eating shall make your count for the lamb.

(Exodus 12:5)
Your lamb shall be without blemish, a male of the first year: you shall take it out from the sheep, or from the goats:

(Exodus 12:6)
And you shall keep it up until the fourteenth day of the same month: and the whole assembly of the congregation of Israel shall kill it in the evening.

(Exodus 12:7)
> And they shall take of the blood, and strike it on the two side posts and on the upper door post of the houses, wherein they shall eat it.

(Exodus 12:8)
> And they shall eat the flesh in that night, roast with fire, and unleavened bread; and with bitter herbs they shall eat it.

(Exodus 12:9)
> Eat not of it raw, nor sodden at all with water, but roast with fire; his head with his legs, and with the inwards thereof.

(Exodus 12:10)
> And you shall let nothing of it remain until the morning; and that which remains of it until the morning you shall burn with fire.

(Exodus 12:11)
> And thus shall you eat it; with your loins girded, your shoes on your feet, and your staff in your hand; and you shall eat it in haste: it is the LORD'S passover.

(Exodus 12:12)
> For I will pass through the land of Egypt this night, and will smite all the firstborn in the land of Egypt, both man and beast; and against all the gods of Egypt I will execute judgment: I am the LORD.

(Exodus 12:13)
> And the blood shall be to you for a token upon the houses where you are: and when I see the blood, I will pass over you, and the plague shall not be upon you to destroy you, when I smite the land of Egypt.

Book Six: From Goshen to Sinai

(Exodus 12:14)
And this day shall be to you for a memorial; and you shall keep it a feast to the LORD throughout your generations; you shall keep it a feast by an ordinance forever.

(Exodus 12:15)
Seven days shall you eat unleavened bread; even the first day you shall put away leaven out of your houses: for whosoever eats leavened bread from the first day until the seventh day, that soul shall be cut off from Israel.

(Exodus 12:16)
And in the first day there shall be a holy convocation, and in the seventh day there shall be an holy convocation to you; no manner of work shall be done in them, save that which every man must eat, that only may be done of you.

(Exodus 12:17)
And you shall observe the feast of unleavened bread; for in this selfsame day have I brought your armies out of the land of Egypt: therefore shall you observe this day in your generations by an ordinance forever.

(Exodus 12:18)
In the first month, on the fourteenth day of the month at even, you shall eat unleavened bread, until the one and twentieth day of the month at even.

(Exodus 12:19)
Seven days shall there be no leaven found in your houses: for whosoever eats that which is leavened, even that soul shall be cut off from the congregation of Israel, whether he be a stranger, or born in the land.

(Exodus 12:20)
You shall eat nothing leavened; in all your habitations shall you eat unleavened bread.

(Exodus 12:21)
Then Moses called for all the elders of Israel, and said to them, Draw out and take you a lamb according to your families, and kill the passover.

(Exodus 12:22)
And you shall take a bunch of hyssop, and dip it in the blood that is in the basin, and strike the lintel and the two side posts with the blood that is in the basin; and none of you shall go out at the door of his house until the morning.

(Exodus 12:23) (...Jasher 80:41)
Celebrate your feast and make your Passover, for behold the LORD will pass through in the midst of the night among all the Egyptians, to smite the Egyptians, all their first born, from the first born of a man to the first born of a beast; and when he sees your Passover, the blood upon the lintel, and on the two side posts, the LORD will pass over the door, and will not suffer the destroyer to come in to your houses to smite you.

(Exodus 12:24)
And you shall observe this thing for an ordinance to you and to your sons forever.

(Exodus 12:25)
And it shall come to pass, when you be come to the land which the LORD will give you, according as he has promised, that you shall keep this service.

Book Six: From Goshen to Sinai

(Exodus 12:26)
And it shall come to pass, when your children shall say to you, What mean you by this service?

(Exodus 12:27)
That you shall say, It is the sacrifice of the LORD'S passover, who passed over the houses of the children of Israel in Egypt, when he smote the Egyptians, and delivered our houses. And the people bowed the head and worshipped.

(Exodus 12:28) (Jasher 80:42)
And the children of Israel went away, and did as the LORD had commanded Moses and Aaron, so they did in that night.

(Exodus 12:29) (Jasher 80:43)
And it came to pass, that at midnight the LORD went forth in the midst of Egypt, and smote all the firstborn in the land of Egypt, from the firstborn of man, Pharaoh that sat on his throne, to the firstborn of the captive that was in the dungeon; and all the firstborn of cattle.

(Exodus 12:30) (Jasher 80:44)
And Pharaoh rose up in the night, he, and all his servants, and all the Egyptians; and there was a great cry in Egypt in that night; for there was not a house where there was not one dead.

(Jasher 80:45)
Also the likenesses of the first born of Egypt, which were carved in the walls at their houses, were destroyed and fell to the ground.

(Jasher 80:46)
Even the bones of their first born who had died before this and

whom they had buried in their houses, were raked up by the dogs of Egypt on that night and dragged before the Egyptians and cast before them.

(Jasher 80:47)
And all the Egyptians saw this evil which had suddenly come upon them, and all the Egyptians cried out with a loud voice.

(Jasher 80:48)
And all the families of Egypt wept upon that night, each man for his son and each man for his daughter, being the first born, and the tumult of Egypt was heard at a distance on that night.

(Jasher 80:49)
And Bathia the daughter of Pharaoh went forth with the king on that night to seek Moses and Aaron in their houses, and they found them in their houses, eating and drinking and rejoicing with all Israel.

(Jasher 80:50)
And Bathia said to Moses, Is this the reward for the good which I have done to you, who have reared you and stretched you out, and you have brought this evil upon me and my father's house?

(Jasher 80:51)
And Moses said to her, Surely ten plagues did the Lord bring upon Egypt; did any evil accrue to you from any of them? Did one of them affect you? And she said, No.

(Jasher 80:52)
And Moses said to her, Although you are the first born to your mother, you shall not die, and no evil shall reach you in the midst of Egypt.

Book Six: From Goshen to Sinai

(Jasher 80:53)
And she said, What advantage is it to me, when I see the king, my brother, and all his household and subjects in this evil, whose first born perish with all the first born of Egypt?

(Jasher 80:54)
And Moses said to her, Surely your brother and his household, and subjects, the families of Egypt, would not hearken to the words of the Lord, therefore did this evil come upon them.

(Jasher 80:55...)
And Pharaoh king of Egypt approached Moses and Aaron, and some of the children of Israel who were with them in that place,

(Exodus 12:31) (...Jasher 80:55, 56...)
And he called for Moses and Aaron by night, and said, Rise up, and take your brothers, and get you forth from among my people, both you and all the children of Israel who are in the land; and go, serve the LORD, as you have said.

(Exodus 12:32) (...Jasher 80:56)
Also take your flocks and your herds, and all belonging to them, they shall leave nothing remaining, as you have said, and be gone; only pray for me to the Lord your God and bless me also.

(Exodus 12:33)
And the Egyptians were urgent upon the people, that they might send them out of the land in haste; for they said, We be all dead men.

(Jasher 80:57)
And Moses said to Pharaoh, Behold though you are your

mother's first born, yet fear not, for you will not die, for the Lord has commanded that you shall live, in order to show you his great might and strong stretched out arm.

(Jasher 80:58)
And Pharaoh ordered the children of Israel to be sent away, and all the Egyptians strengthened themselves to send them, for they said, We are all perishing.

(Exodus 12:34)
And the people took their dough before it was leavened, their kneading troughs being bound up in their clothes upon their shoulders.

(Jasher 80:59)
And all the Egyptians sent the Israelites forth, with great riches, sheep and oxen and precious things, according to the oath of the Lord between him and our Father Abraham.

(Jasher 80:60)
And the children of Israel delayed going forth at night, and when the Egyptians came to them to bring them out, they said to them, Are we thieves, that we should go forth at night?

(Exodus 12:35)
And the children of Israel did according to the word of Moses; and they borrowed of the Egyptians jewels of silver, and jewels of gold, and raiment:

(Exodus 12:36) (Jasher 80:61)
And the LORD gave the people favor in the sight of the Egyptians, so that they lent to them such things as they required. And the children of Israel asked of the Egyptians, vessels of silver, and vessels of gold, and garments, and the

children of Israel stripped the Egyptians. And they spoiled the Egyptians.

(Jasher 80:62)
And Moses hastened and rose up and went to the river of Egypt, and brought up from there the coffin of Joseph and took it with him.

(Jasher 80:63)
The children of Israel also brought up, each man his father's coffin with him, and each man the coffins of his tribe.

(Exodus 12:37)
And the children of Israel journeyed from Rameses to Succoth, about six hundred thousand on foot that were men, beside children.

(Exodus 12:38)
And a mixed multitude went up also with them; and flocks, and herds, even very much cattle.

(Exodus 12:39)
And they baked unleavened cakes of the dough which they brought forth out of Egypt, for it was not leavened; because they were thrust out of Egypt, and could not tarry, neither had they prepared for themselves any victual.

(Exodus 12:40)
Now the sojourning of the children of Israel, who dwelt in Egypt, was four hundred and thirty years.

(Exodus 12:41)
And it came to pass at the end of the four hundred and thirty years, even the selfsame day it came to pass, that all the hosts

of the LORD went out from the land of Egypt.

(Exodus 12:42)
It is a night to be much observed to the LORD for bringing them out from the land of Egypt: this is that night of the LORD to be observed of all the children of Israel in their generations.

(Exodus 12:43)
And the LORD said to Moses and Aaron, This is the ordinance of the passover: There shall no stranger eat thereof:

(Exodus 12:44)
But every man's servant that is bought for money, when you have circumcised him, then shall he eat thereof.

(Exodus 12:45)
A foreigner and an hired servant shall not eat thereof.

(Exodus 12:46)
In one house shall it be eaten; you shall not carry forth ought of the flesh abroad out of the house; neither shall you break a bone thereof.

(Exodus 12:47)
All the congregation of Israel shall keep it.

(Exodus 12:48)
And when a stranger shall sojourn with you, and will keep the passover to the LORD, let all his males be circumcised, and then let him come near and keep it; and he shall be as one that is born in the land: for no uncircumcised person shall eat thereof.

(Exodus 12:49)
One law shall be to him that is homeborn, and to the stranger that sojourns among you.

(Exodus 12:50)
Thus did all the children of Israel; as the LORD commanded Moses and Aaron, so did they.

(Exodus 12:51)
And it came to pass the selfsame day, that the LORD did bring the children of Israel out of the land of Egypt by their armies.

(Jubilees 49:1)
Remember the commandment which the Lord commanded you concerning the Passover, that you should celebrate it in its season on the fourteenth of the first month, that you should kill it before it is evening, and that they should eat it by night on the evening of the fifteenth from the time of the setting of the sun.

(Jubilees 49:2)
For on this night - the beginning of the festival and the beginning of the joy - you were eating the Passover in Egypt, when all the powers of Mastêmâ had been let loose to slay all the first-born in the land of Egypt, from the first-born of Pharaoh to the first-born of the captive maid-servant in the mill, and to the cattle.

(Jubilees 49:3)
And this is the sign which the Lord gave them: Into every house on the lintels of which they saw the blood of a lamb of the first year, into that house they should not enter to slay, but should pass by it, that all those should be saved that were in the house because the sign of the blood was on its lintels.

(Jubilees 49:4)
And the powers of the Lord did everything according as the Lord commanded them, and they passed by all the children of Israel, and the plague came not on them to destroy from amongst them any soul either of cattle, or man, or dog.

(Jubilees 49:5)
And the plague was very grievous in Egypt, and there was no house in Egypt where there was not one dead, and weeping and lamentation.

(Jubilees 49:6)
And all Israel was eating the flesh of the paschal lamb, and drinking the wine, and was lauding, and blessing, and giving thanks to the Lord God of their fathers, and was ready to go forth from under the yoke of Egypt, and from the evil bondage.

(Jubilees 49:7)
And remember you this day all the days of your life, and observe it from year to year all the days of your life, once a year, on its day, according to all the law thereof, and do not adjourn it from day today, or from month to month.

(Jubilees 49:8)
For it is an eternal ordinance, and engraved on the heavenly tablets regarding all the children of Israel that they should observe it every year on its day once a year, throughout all their generations; and there is no limit of days, for this is ordained forever.

(Jubilees 49:9)
And the man who is free from uncleanness, and does not come to observe it on occasion of its day, so as to bring an acceptable offering before the Lord, and to eat and to drink

before the Lord on the day of its festival, that man who is clean and close at hand shall be cut off: because he offered not the oblation of the Lord in its appointed season, he shall take the guilt on himself.

(Jubilees 49:10)
Let the children of Israel come and observe the Passover on the day of its fixed time, on the fourteenth day of the first month, between the evenings, from the third part of the day to the third part of the night, for two portions of the day are given to the light, and a third part to the evening.

(Jubilees 49:11)
This is that which the Lord commanded you that you should observe it between the evenings.

(Jubilees 49:12)
And it is not permissible to slay it during any period of the light, but during the period bordering on the evening, and let them eat it at the time of the evening, until the third part of the night, and whatever is left over of all its flesh from the third part of the night and onwards, let them burn it with fire.

(Jubilees 49:13)
And they shall not cook it with water, nor shall they eat it raw, but roast on the fire: they shall eat it with diligence, its head with the inwards thereof and its feet they shall roast with fire, and not break any bone thereof; for of the children of Israel no bone shall be crushed.

(Jubilees 49:14)
For this reason, the Lord commanded the children of Israel to observe the Passover on the day of its fixed time, and they shall not break a bone thereof; for it is a festival day, and a

day commanded, and there may be no passing over from day today, and month to month, but on the day of its festival let it be observed.

(Jubilees 49:15)
And do you command the children of Israel to observe the Passover throughout their days, every year, once a year on the day of its fixed time, and it shall come for a memorial well pleasing before the Lord, and no plague shall come on them to slay or to smite in that year in which they celebrate the Passover in its season in every respect according to His command.

(Jubilees 49:16)
And they shall not eat it outside the sanctuary of the Lord, but before the sanctuary of the Lord, and all the people of the congregation of Israel shall celebrate it in its appointed season.

(Jubilees 49:17)
And every man who has come on its day shall eat it in the sanctuary of your God before the Lord from twenty years old and upward; for thus is it written and ordained that they should eat it in the sanctuary of the Lord.

(Jubilees 49:18)
And when the children of Israel come into the land which they are to possess, into the land of Canaan, and set up the tabernacle of the Lord in the midst of the land in one of their tribes until the sanctuary of the Lord has been built in the land, let them come and celebrate the Passover in the midst of the tabernacle of the Lord, and let them slay it before the Lord from year to year.

(Jubilees 49:19)
And in the days when the house has been built in the name of the Lord in the land of their inheritance, they shall go there and slay the Passover in the evening, at sunset, at the third part of the day.

(Jubilees 49:20)
And they shall offer its blood on the threshold of the altar, and shall place its fat on the fire which is on the altar, and they shall eat its flesh roasted with fire in the court of the house which has been sanctified in the name of the Lord.

(Jubilees 49:21)
And they may not celebrate the Passover in their cities, nor in any place save before the tabernacle of the Lord, or before His house where His name has dwelt; and they shall not go astray from the Lord.

(Jubilees 49:22)
And do you, Moses, command the children of Israel to observe the ordinances of the Passover, as it was commanded to you; declare you to them every year and the day of its days, and the festival of unleavened bread, that they should eat unleavened bread seven days, and that they should observe its festival, and that they bring an oblation every day during those seven days of joy before the Lord on the altar of your God.

(Jubilees 49:23)
For you celebrated this festival with haste when you went forth from Egypt till you entered into the wilderness of Shur; for on the shore of the sea you completed it.

The History of Ancient Israel

Exodus: Chapter Thirteen

(Exodus 13:1)
    And the LORD spoke to Moses, saying,

(Jubilees 48:4)
I delivered you out of the hand of prince Mastêmâ, and you did perform the signs and wonders which you were sent to perform in Egypt against Pharaoh, and against all his house, and against his servants and his people.

(Jubilees 48:5)
And the Lord executed a great vengeance on them for Israel's sake, and smote them through blood and frogs, lice and dog-flies, and malignant boils breaking forth in blains; and their cattle by death; and by hail-stones, thereby He destroyed everything that grew for them; and by locusts which devoured the residue which had been left by the hail, and by darkness; and by the death of the first-born of men and animals, and on all their idols the Lord took vengeance and burned them with fire.

(Jubilees 48:6)
And everything was sent through your hand, that you should declare these things before they were done, and you did speak with the king of Egypt before all his servants and before his people.

(Jubilees 48:7)
And everything took place according to your words; ten great and terrible judgments came on the land of Egypt that you might execute vengeance on it for Israel.

(Jubilees 48:8)
And the Lord did everything for Israel's sake, and according to His covenant, which he had ordained with Abraham that He would take vengeance on them as they had brought them by force into bondage.

(Jubilees 48:9)
And the prince Mastêmâ stood up against you, and sought to cast you into the hands of Pharaoh, and he helped the Egyptian sorcerers,

(Jubilees 48:10)
And they stood up and wrought before you the evils indeed we permitted them to work, but the remedies we did not allow to be wrought by their hands.

(Jubilees 48:11)
And the Lord smote them with malignant ulcers, and they were not able to stand, for we destroyed them so that they could not perform a single sign.

(Exodus 13:2)
Sanctify to me all the firstborn, whatsoever opens the womb among the children of Israel, both of man and of beast: it is mine.

(Exodus 13:3)
And Moses said to the people, Remember this day, in which you came out from Egypt, out of the house of bondage; for by

strength of hand the LORD brought you out from this place: there shall no leavened bread be eaten.

(Exodus 13:4)
This day came you out in the month Abib.

(Exodus 13:5)
And it shall be when the LORD shall bring you into the land of the Canaanites, and the Hittites, and the Amorites, and the Hivites, and the Jebusites, which he swore to your fathers to give you, a land flowing with milk and honey, that you shall keep this service in this month.

(Exodus 13:6)
Seven days you shall eat unleavened bread, and in the seventh day shall be a feast to the LORD.

(Exodus 13:7)
Unleavened bread shall be eaten seven days; and there shall no leavened bread be seen with you, neither shall there be leaven seen with you in all your quarters.

(Exodus 13:8)
And you shall shew your son in that day, saying, This is done because of that which the LORD did to me when I came forth out of Egypt.

(Exodus 13:9)
And it shall be for a sign to you upon your hand, and for a memorial between your eyes, that the LORD'S law may be in your mouth: for with a strong hand has the LORD brought you out of Egypt.

(Exodus 13:10)
You shall therefore keep this ordinance in his season from year to year.

(Exodus 13:11)
And it shall be when the LORD shall bring you into the land of the Canaanites, as he swore to you and to your fathers, and shall give it you,

(Exodus 13:12)
That you shall set apart to the LORD all that opens the matrix, and every firstling that comes of a beast which you have; the males shall be the LORD'S.

(Exodus 13:13)
And every firstling of a donkey you shall redeem with a lamb; and if you will not redeem it, then you shall break his neck: and all the firstborn of man among your children shall you redeem.

(Exodus 13:14)
And it shall be when your son asks you in time to come, saying, What is this? That you shall say to him, By strength of hand the LORD brought us out from Egypt, from the house of bondage:

(Exodus 13:15)
And it came to pass, when Pharaoh would hardly let us go, that the LORD slew all the firstborn in the land of Egypt, both the firstborn of man, and the firstborn of beast: therefore I sacrifice to the LORD all that opens the matrix, being males; but all the firstborn of my children I redeem.

(Exodus 13:16)
And it shall be for a token upon your hand, and for frontlets between your eyes: for by strength of hand the LORD brought us forth out of Egypt.

(Exodus 13:17)
And it came to pass, when Pharaoh had let the people go, that God led them not through the way of the land of the Philistines, although that was near; for God said, Lest peradventure the people repent when they see war, and they return to Egypt:

(Exodus 13:18)
But God led the people about, through the way of the wilderness of the Red sea: and the children of Israel went up harnessed out of the land of Egypt.

(Exodus 13:19)
And Moses took the bones of Joseph with him: for he had straitly sworn the children of Israel, saying, God will surely visit you; and you shall carry up my bones away hence with you.

(Jasher 81:1)
And the children of Israel journeyed from Rameses to Succoth, about six hundred thousand men on foot, besides the little ones and their wives.

(Jasher 81:2)
Also a mixed multitude went up with them, and flocks and herds, even much cattle.

(Jasher 81:3)
And the sojourning of the children of Israel, who dwelt in the land of Egypt in hard labor, was two hundred and ten years.

(Jasher 81:4)
And at the end of two hundred and ten years, the Lord brought forth the children of Israel from Egypt with a strong hand.

(Jasher 81:5)
And the children of Israel traveled from Egypt and from Goshen and from Rameses, and encamped in Succoth on the fifteenth day of the first month.

(Jasher 81:6)
And the Egyptians buried all their first born whom the Lord had smitten, and all the Egyptians buried their slain for three days.

(Exodus 13:20) (Jasher 81:7)
And they took their journey from Succoth, and encamped in Etham, in the edge of the wilderness.

(Exodus 13:21)
And the LORD went before them by day in a pillar of a cloud, to lead them the way; and by night in a pillar of fire, to give them light; to go by day and night:

(Exodus 13:22)
He took not away the pillar of the cloud by day, nor the pillar of fire by night, from before the people.

Exodus: Chapter Fourteen

(Exodus 14:1)
And the LORD spoke to Moses, saying,

(Exodus 14:2)
Speak to the children of Israel, that they turn and encamp before Pihahiroth, between Migdol and the sea, over against Baalzephon: before it shall you encamp by the sea.

(Exodus 14:3)
For Pharaoh will say of the children of Israel, They are entangled in the land, the wilderness has shut them in.

(Exodus 14:4)
And I will harden Pharaoh's heart, that he shall follow after them; and I will be honored upon Pharaoh, and upon all his host; that the Egyptians may know that I am the LORD. And they did so.

(Jasher 81:6)
And the Egyptians buried all their first born whom the Lord had smitten, and all the Egyptians buried their slain for three days.

(Jasher 81:7)
And the children of Israel traveled from Succoth and encamped in Ethom, at the end of the wilderness.

(Jasher 81:8)
And on the third day after the Egyptians had buried their first born, many men rose up from Egypt and went after Israel to make them return to Egypt, for they repented that they had sent the Israelites away from their servitude.

(Jasher 81:9)
And one man said to his neighbor, Surely Moses and Aaron spoke to Pharaoh, saying, We will go a three days' journey in the wilderness and sacrifice to the Lord our God.

(Jasher 81:10)
Now therefore let us rise up early in the morning and cause them to return, and it shall be that if they return with us to Egypt to their masters, then shall we know that there is faith in them, but if they will not return, then will we fight with them, and make them come back with great power and a strong hand.

(Jasher 81:11)
And all the nobles of Pharaoh rose up in the morning, and with them about seven hundred thousand men, and they went forth from Egypt on that day, and came to the place where the children of Israel were.

(Jasher 81:12)
And all the Egyptians saw and behold Moses and Aaron and all the children of Israel were sitting before Pi-hahiroth, eating and drinking and celebrating the feast of the Lord.

(Jasher 81:13)
And all the Egyptians said to the children of Israel, Surely you said, We will go a journey for three days in the wilderness and sacrifice to our God and return.

Book Six: From Goshen to Sinai

(Jasher 81:14)
Now therefore this day makes five days since you went, why do you not return to your masters?

(Jasher 81:15)
And Moses and Aaron answered them, saying, Because the Lord our God has testified in us, saying, You shall no more return to Egypt, but we will betake ourselves to a land flowing with milk and honey, as the Lord our God had sworn to our ancestors to give to us.

(Jasher 81:16)
And when the nobles of Egypt saw that the children of Israel did not hearken to them, to return to Egypt, they girded themselves to fight with Israel.

(Jasher 81:17)
And the Lord strengthened the hearts of the children of Israel over the Egyptians, that they gave them a severe beating, and the battle was sore upon the Egyptians, and all the Egyptians fled from before the children of Israel, for many of them perished by the hand of Israel.

(Jubilees 48:12)
And notwithstanding all (these) signs and wonders the prince Mastêmâ was not put to shame because he took courage and cried to the Egyptians to pursue after you with all the powers of the Egyptians, with their chariots, and with their horses, and with all the hosts of the peoples of Egypt.

(Exodus 14:5...) (Jasher 81:18, 19...)
And the nobles of Pharaoh went to Egypt and told Pharaoh, saying, The children of Israel have fled, and will no more return to Egypt, and in this manner did Moses and Aaron

speak to us. And the heart of Pharaoh and of his servants was turned against the people.

(...Jasher 81:19)
And they repented that they had sent Israel; and all the Egyptians advised Pharaoh to pursue the children of Israel to make them come back to their burdens.

(...Exodus 14:5) (Jasher 81:20)
And they said, Why have we done this, that we have let Israel go from serving us?

(Jasher 81:21)
And the Lord strengthened the hearts of all the Egyptians to pursue the Israelites, for the Lord desired to overthrow the Egyptians in the Red Sea.

(Exodus 14:6) (Jasher 81:22)
And Pharaoh rose up and made ready his chariot, and he ordered all the Egyptians to assemble, not one man was left excepting the little ones and the women, and he took his people with him:

(Jasher 81:23)
And all the Egyptians went forth with Pharaoh to pursue the children of Israel, and the camp of Egypt was an exceedingly large and heavy camp, about ten hundred thousand men.

(Exodus 14:7)
And he took six hundred chosen chariots, and all the chariots of Egypt, and captains over every one of them.

(Jasher 81:24...)
And the whole of this camp went and pursued the children of

Book Six: From Goshen to Sinai

Israel to bring them back to Egypt.

(Exodus 14:8)
And the LORD hardened the heart of Pharaoh king of Egypt, and he pursued after the children of Israel: and the children of Israel went out with a high hand.

(Exodus 14:9) (...Jasher 81:24)
But the Egyptians pursued after them, all the horses and chariots of Pharaoh, and his horsemen, and his army, and overtook them encamping by the Red sea, beside Pihahiroth, before Baalzephon.

(Exodus 14:10) (Jasher 81:25)
And when Pharaoh drew nigh, the children of Israel lifted up their eyes, and, behold, the Egyptians marched after them; and they were sore afraid: and the children of Israel cried out to the LORD.

(Exodus 14:11)
And they said to Moses, Because there were no graves in Egypt, have you taken us away to die in the wilderness? Why have you dealt thus with us, to carry us forth out of Egypt?

(Exodus 14:12)
Is not this the word that we did tell you in Egypt, saying, Let us alone, that we may serve the Egyptians? For it had been better for us to serve the Egyptians, than that we should die in the wilderness.

(Jasher 81:26)
And on account of the Egyptians, the children of Israel divided themselves into four divisions, and they were divided in their

opinions, for they were afraid of the Egyptians, and Moses spoke to each of them.

(Jasher 81:27)
The first division was of the children of Reuben, Simeon, and Issachar, and they resolved to cast themselves into the sea, for they were exceedingly afraid of the Egyptians.

(Exodus 14:13...) (Jasher 81:28)
And Moses said to the people, Do not fear, stand still, and see the salvation of the LORD, which he will shew to you today:

(Jasher 81:29)
The second division was of the children of Zebulun, Benjamin and Naphtali, and they resolved to go back to Egypt with the Egyptians.

(...Exodus 14:13) (Jasher 81:30)
And Moses said to them, Fear not, for the Egyptians whom you have seen today, you shall see them again no more forever.

(Jasher 81:31)
The third division was of the children of Judah and Joseph, and they resolved to go to meet the Egyptians to fight with them.

(Exodus 14:14) (Jasher 81:32)
And Moses said to them, Stand in your places, for the LORD shall fight for you, and you shall hold your peace.

(Jasher 81:33)
And the fourth division was of the children of Levi, Gad, and Asher, and they resolved to go into the midst of the Egyptians to confound them, and Moses said to them, Remain in your

stations and fear not, only call to the Lord that he may save you out of their hands.

(Jasher 81:34)
After this Moses rose up from amidst the people, and he prayed to the Lord and said,

(Jasher 81:35)
O Lord God of the whole earth, save now your people whom you did bring forth from Egypt, and let not the Egyptians boast that power and might are theirs.

(Exodus 14:15) (Jasher 81:36...)
And the LORD said to Moses, Why do you cry to me? Speak to the children of Israel, that they go forward:

(Exodus 14:16) (...Jasher 81:36)
But lift you up your rod, and stretch out your hand over the sea, and divide it: and the children of Israel shall go on dry ground through the midst of the sea.

(Exodus 14:17)
And I, behold, I will harden the hearts of the Egyptians, and they shall follow them: and I will get me honor upon Pharaoh, and upon all his host, upon his chariots, and upon his horsemen.

(Exodus 14:18)
And the Egyptians shall know that I am the LORD, when I have gotten me honor upon Pharaoh, upon his chariots, and upon his horsemen.

(Exodus 14:19)
And the angel of God, which went before the camp of Israel,

removed and went behind them; and the pillar of the cloud went from before their face, and stood behind them:

(Exodus 14:20)
And it came between the camp of the Egyptians and the camp of Israel; and it was a cloud and darkness to them, but it gave light by night to these: so that the one came not near the other all the night.

(Exodus 14:21) (Jasher 81:37)
And Moses stretched out his hand over the sea; and the LORD caused the sea to go back by a strong east wind all that night, and made the sea dry land, and the waters were divided.

(Exodus 14:22) (Jasher 81:38)
And the waters of the sea were divided into twelve parts, and the children of Israel went into the midst of the sea upon the dry ground and the children of Israel passed through on foot, with shoes, as a man would pass through a prepared road: and the waters were a wall to them on their right hand, and on their left.

(Jasher 81:39)
And the Lord manifested to the children of Israel his wonders in Egypt and in the sea by the hand of Moses and Aaron.

(Exodus 14:23) (Jasher 81:40...)
And when the children of Israel had entered the sea, the Egyptians pursued, and went in after them to the midst of the sea, even all Pharaoh's horses, his chariots, and his horsemen.

(Exodus 14:24)
And it came to pass, that in the morning watch the LORD looked to the host of the Egyptians through the pillar of fire

and of the cloud, and troubled the host of the Egyptians,

(Exodus 14:25)
And took off their chariot wheels, that they drove them heavily: so that the Egyptians said, Let us flee from the face of Israel; for the LORD fights for them against the Egyptians.

(Exodus 14:26)
And the LORD said to Moses, Stretch out your hand over the sea, that the waters may come again upon the Egyptians, upon their chariots, and upon their horsemen.

(Exodus 14:27)
And Moses stretched forth his hand over the sea, and the sea returned to his strength when the morning appeared; and the Egyptians fled against it; and the LORD overthrew the Egyptians in the midst of the sea.

(Exodus 14:28) (...Jasher 81:40)
And the waters of the sea returned and resumed upon them, and covered the chariots, and the horsemen, and all the host of Pharaoh that came into the sea after them; and they all sank in the water, and there remained not so much as one of them excepting Pharaoh, who gave thanks to the Lord and believed in him, therefore the Lord did not cause him to perish at that time with the Egyptians.

(Jasher 81:41)
And the Lord ordered an angel to take him from among the Egyptians, who cast him upon the land of Ninevah and he reigned over it for a long time.

(Exodus 14:29) (Jubilees 48:13)
But the Lord stood between the Egyptians and Israel, and they

delivered Israel out of Pharaoh's hand, and out of the hand of his people, and the Lord brought the children of Israel walked upon dry land in the midst of the sea; and the waters were a wall to them on their right hand, and on their left.

(Exodus 14:30) (Jasher 81:42...)
Thus the LORD saved Israel that day out of the hand of the Egyptians; and Israel saw the Egyptians dead upon the sea shore.

(Exodus 14:31) (...Jasher 81:42)
And Israel saw that great work which the LORD did upon the Egyptians in the sea: and the people feared the LORD, and believed the LORD, and his servant Moses.

(Jubilees 48:14)
And all the peoples whom he brought to pursue after Israel, the Lord our God cast them into the midst of the sea, into the depths of the abyss beneath the children of Israel, even as the people of Egypt had cast their children into the river He took vengeance on 1,000,000 of them, and one thousand strong and energetic men were destroyed on account of one suckling of the children of your people which they had thrown into the river.

(Jubilees 48:15)
And on the fourteenth day and on the fifteenth and on the sixteenth and on the seventeenth and on the eighteenth the prince Mastêmâ was bound and imprisoned behind the children of Israel that he might not accuse them.

(Jubilees 48:16)
And on the nineteenth, we let them loose that they might help the Egyptians and pursue the children of Israel.

(Jubilees 48:17)
And he hardened their hearts and made them stubborn, and the device was devised by the Lord our God that He might smite the Egyptians and cast them into the sea.

(Jubilees 48:18)
And on the fourteenth, we bound him that he might not accuse the children of Israel on the day when they asked the Egyptians for vessels and garments, vessels of silver, and vessels of gold, and vessels of bronze, in order to despoil the Egyptians in return for the bondage in which they had forced them to serve.

(Jubilees 48:19)
And we did not lead forth the children of Israel from Egypt empty handed.

The History of Ancient Israel

Exodus: Chapter Fifteen

(Exodus 15:1) (Jasher 81:43)
>Then sang Moses and the children of Israel this song to the LORD, on the day when the Lord caused the Egyptians to fall before them and spoke, saying, I will sing to the LORD, for he has triumphed gloriously: the horse and his rider has he thrown into the sea.

(Exodus 15:2)
>The LORD is my strength and song, and he is become my salvation: he is my God, and I will prepare him a habitation; my father's God, and I will exalt him.

(Exodus 15:3)
>The LORD is a man of war: the LORD is his name.

(Exodus 15:4)
>Pharaoh's chariots and his host has he cast into the sea: his chosen captains also are drowned in the Red sea.

(Exodus 15:5)
>The depths have covered them: they sank into the bottom as a stone.

(Exodus 15:6)
>Your right hand, O LORD, is become glorious in power: your right hand, O LORD, has dashed in pieces the enemy.

(Exodus 15:7)
    And in the greatness of your excellency you have overthrown them that rose up against you: you sent forth your wrath, which consumed them as stubble.

(Exodus 15:8)
    And with the blast of your nostrils the waters were gathered together, the floods stood upright as a heap, and the depths were congealed in the heart of the sea.

(Exodus 15:9)
    The enemy said, I will pursue, I will overtake, I will divide the spoil; my lust shall be satisfied upon them; I will draw my sword, my hand shall destroy them.

(Exodus 15:10)
    You blew with your wind, the sea covered them: they sank as lead in the mighty waters.

(Exodus 15:11)
    Who is like to you, O LORD, among the gods? Who is like you, glorious in holiness, fearful in praises, doing wonders?

(Exodus 15:12)
    You stretched out your right hand, the earth swallowed them.

(Exodus 15:13)
    You in your mercy have led forth the people which you have redeemed: you have guided them in your strength to your holy habitation.

(Exodus 15:14)
    The people shall hear, and be afraid: sorrow shall take hold on the inhabitants of Palestina.

Book Six: From Goshen to Sinai

(Exodus 15:15)
>Then the dukes of Edom shall be amazed; the mighty men of Moab, trembling shall take hold upon them; all the inhabitants of Canaan shall melt away.

(Exodus 15:16)
>Fear and dread shall fall upon them; by the greatness of your arm they shall be as still as a stone; till your people pass over, O LORD, till the people pass over, which you have purchased.

(Exodus 15:17)
>You shall bring them in, and plant them in the mountain of your inheritance, in the place, O LORD, which you have made for you to dwell in, in the Sanctuary, O Lord, which your hands have established.

(Exodus 15:18)
>The LORD shall reign forever and ever.

(Exodus 15:19)
>For the horse of Pharaoh went in with his chariots and with his horsemen into the sea, and the LORD brought again the waters of the sea upon them; but the children of Israel went on dry land in the midst of the sea.

(Exodus 15:20)
>And Miriam the prophetess, the sister of Aaron, took a timbrel in her hand; and all the women went out after her with timbrels and with dances.

(Exodus 15:21)
>And Miriam answered them, Sing to the LORD, for he has triumphed gloriously; the horse and his rider has he thrown into the sea.

(Jasher 81:44)
And all Israel sang in concert, saying, I will sing to the Lord for He is greatly exalted, the horse and his rider has he cast into the sea; behold it is written in the book of the law of God.

(Exodus 15:22)
So Moses brought Israel from the Red sea, and they went out into the wilderness of Shur; and they went three days in the wilderness, and found no water.

(Exodus 15:23) (Jasher 81:45...)
After this the children of Israel proceeded on their journey, and encamped in Marah. And when they came to Marah, they could not drink of the waters of Marah, for they were bitter: therefore the name of it was called Marah.

(Exodus 15:24)
And the people murmured against Moses, saying, What shall we drink?

(Exodus 15:25)
And he cried to the LORD; and the LORD shewed him a tree, which when he had cast into the waters, the waters were made sweet: there he made for them a statute and an ordinance, and there he proved them,

(...Jasher 81:45)
And the Lord gave to the children of Israel statutes and judgments in that place in Marah, and the Lord commanded the children of Israel to walk in all his ways and to serve him.

(Exodus 15:26)
And said, If you will diligently hearken to the voice of the LORD your God, and will do that which is right in his sight,

and will give ear to his commandments, and keep all his statutes, I will put none of these diseases upon you, which I have brought upon the Egyptians: for I am the LORD that heals you.

(Exodus 15:27) (Jasher 81:46)
And they journeyed from Marah and came to Elim, where were twelve wells of water, and threescore and ten date palm trees: and they encamped there by the waters.

The History of Ancient Israel

Exodus: Chapter Sixteen

(Exodus 16:1) (Jasher 81:47)
 And they took their journey from Elim, and all the congregation of the children of Israel came to the wilderness of Sin, which is between Elim and Sinai, on the fifteenth day of the second month after their departing out of the land of Egypt.

(Exodus 16:2)
 And the whole congregation of the children of Israel murmured against Moses and Aaron in the wilderness:

(Exodus 16:3)
 And the children of Israel said to them, Would to God we had died by the hand of the LORD in the land of Egypt, when we sat by the flesh pots, and when we did eat bread to the full; for you have brought us forth into this wilderness, to kill this whole assembly with hunger.

(Exodus 16:4)
 Then said the LORD to Moses, Behold, I will rain bread from heaven for you; and the people shall go out and gather a certain rate every day, that I may prove them, whether they will walk in my law, or no.

(Exodus 16:5)
 And it shall come to pass, that on the sixth day they shall prepare that which they bring in; and it shall be twice as much as they gather daily.

(Exodus 16:6)
> And Moses and Aaron said to all the children of Israel, At even, then you shall know that the LORD has brought you out from the land of Egypt:

(Exodus 16:7)
> And in the morning, then you shall see the glory of the LORD; for that he hears your murmurings against the LORD: and what are we, that you murmur against us?

(Exodus 16:8)
> And Moses said, This shall be, when the LORD shall give you in the evening flesh to eat, and in the morning bread to the full; for that the LORD hears your murmurings which you murmur against him: and what are we? Your murmurings are not against us, but against the LORD.

(Exodus 16:9)
> And Moses spoke to Aaron, Say to all the congregation of the children of Israel, Come near before the LORD: for he has heard your murmurings.

(Exodus 16:10)
> And it came to pass, as Aaron spoke to the whole congregation of the children of Israel, that they looked toward the wilderness, and, behold, the glory of the LORD appeared in the cloud.

(Exodus 16:11)
> And the LORD spoke to Moses, saying,

(Exodus 16:12)
> I have heard the murmurings of the children of Israel: speak to them, saying, At even you shall eat flesh, and in the morning you shall be filled with bread; and you shall know that I am the LORD your God.

(Exodus 16:13)
And it came to pass, that at even the quails came up, and covered the camp: and in the morning the dew lay round about the host.

(Exodus 16:14)
And when the dew that lay was gone up, behold, upon the face of the wilderness there lay a small round thing, as small as the hoar frost on the ground.

(Jasher 81:48)
At that time the Lord gave the manna to the children of Israel to eat, and the Lord caused food to rain from heaven for the children of Israel day by day.

(Exodus 16:15)
And when the children of Israel saw it, they said one to another, It is manna: for they knew not what it was. And Moses said to them, This is the bread which the LORD has given you to eat.

(Exodus 16:16)
This is the thing which the LORD has commanded, Gather of it every man according to his eating, an omer for every man, according to the number of your persons; take every man for them which are in his tents.

(Exodus 16:17)
And the children of Israel did so, and gathered, some more, some less.

(Exodus 16:18)
And when they did mete it with an omer, he that gathered much had nothing over, and he that gathered little had no lack; they gathered every man according to his eating.

(Exodus 16:19)
>And Moses said, Let no man leave of it till the morning.

(Exodus 16:20)
>Notwithstanding they hearkened not to Moses; but some of them left of it until the morning, and it bred worms, and stank: and Moses was wroth with them.

(Exodus 16:21)
>And they gathered it every morning, every man according to his eating: and when the sun waxed hot, it melted.

(Exodus 16:22)
>And it came to pass, that on the sixth day they gathered twice as much bread, two omers for one man: and all the rulers of the congregation came and told Moses.

(Exodus 16:23)
>And he said to them, This is that which the LORD has said, Tomorrow is the rest of the holy sabbath to the LORD: bake that which you will bake today, and seethe that you will seethe; and that which remains over lay up for you to be kept until the morning.

(Exodus 16:24)
>And they laid it up till the morning, as Moses bade: and it did not stink, neither was there any worm therein.

(Exodus 16:25)
>And Moses said, Eat that today; for today is a sabbath to the LORD: today you shall not find it in the field.

(Exodus 16:26)
>Six days you shall gather it; but on the seventh day, which is

the sabbath, in it there shall be none.

(Exodus 16:27)
And it came to pass, that there went out some of the people on the seventh day for to gather, and they found none.

(Exodus 16:28)
And the LORD said to Moses, How long will you refuse to keep my commandments and my laws?

(Exodus 16:29)
See, for that the LORD has given you the sabbath, therefore he gives you on the sixth day the bread of two days; abide every man in his place, let no man go out of his place on the seventh day.

(Exodus 16:30)
So the people rested on the seventh day.

(Exodus 16:31)
And the house of Israel called the name thereof Manna: and it was like coriander seed, white; and the taste of it was like wafers made with honey.

(Exodus 16:32)
And Moses said, This is the thing which the LORD commands, Fill an omer of it to be kept for your generations; that they may see the bread wherewith I have fed you in the wilderness, when I brought you forth from the land of Egypt.

(Exodus 16:33)
And Moses said to Aaron, Take a pot, and put an omer full of manna therein, and lay it up before the LORD, to be kept for your generations.

(Exodus 16:34)
As the LORD commanded Moses, so Aaron laid it up before the Testimony, to be kept.

(Exodus 16:35) (Jasher 81:49)
And the children of Israel did eat manna forty years, until they came to a land inhabited; they did eat manna, until they came to the borders of the land of Canaan to possess it.

(Exodus 16:36)
Now an omer is the tenth part of an ephah.

(Jubilees 50:1)
And after this law I made known to you the days of the Sabbaths in the desert of Sinai, which is between Elim and Sinai.

(Jubilees 50:2)
And I told you of the Sabbaths of the land on Mount Sinai, and I told you of the jubilee years in the sabbaths of years: but the year thereof have I not told you till you enter the land which you are to possess.

(Jubilees 50:3)
And the land also shall keep its sabbaths while they dwell on it, and they shall know the jubilee year.

(Jubilees 50:4)
Wherefore I have ordained for you the year-weeks and the years and the jubilees: there are forty-nine jubilees from the days of Adam until this day, and one week and two years: and there are yet forty years to come for learning the commandments of the Lord, until they pass over into the land of Canaan, crossing the Jordan to the west.

(Jubilees 50:5)
And the jubilees shall pass by, until Israel is cleansed from all guilt of fornication, and uncleanness, and pollution, and sin, and error, and dwells with confidence in all the land, and there shall be no more a Satan or any evil one, and the land shall be clean from that time forevermore.

The History of Ancient Israel

Exodus: Chapter Seventeen

(Exodus 17:1) (Jasher 81:50, 51)
    And all the congregation of the children of Israel journeyed from the wilderness of Sin, after their journeys, according to the commandment of the LORD, and encamped in Alush. And they proceeded from Alush and pitched in Rephidim: and there was no water for the people to drink.

(Exodus 17:2)
    Why the people did chide with Moses, and said, Give us water that we may drink. And Moses said to them, Why chide with me? Why do you tempt the LORD?

(Exodus 17:3)
    And the people thirsted there for water; and the people murmured against Moses, and said, Why is this that you have brought us up out of Egypt, to kill us and our children and our cattle with thirst?

(Exodus 17:4)
    And Moses cried to the LORD, saying, What shall I do to this people? They be almost ready to stone me.

(Exodus 17:5)
    And the LORD said to Moses, Go on before the people, and take with you of the elders of Israel; and your rod, wherewith you smote the river, take in your hand, and go.

(Exodus 17:6)
> Behold, I will stand before you there upon the rock in Horeb; and you shall smite the rock, and there shall come water out of it, that the people may drink. And Moses did so in the sight of the elders of Israel.

(Exodus 17:7)
> And he called the name of the place Massah, and Meribah, because of the chiding of the children of Israel, and because they tempted the LORD, saying, Is the LORD among us, or not?

(Exodus 17:8) (Jasher 81:52)
> Then Amalek, the son of Eliphaz, the son of Esau, the brother of Zepho, came and fought with Israel in Rephidim.

(Jasher 81:53)
> And he brought with him eight hundred and one thousand men, magicians and conjurers, and he prepared for battle with Israel in Rephidim.

(Exodus 17:9)
> And Moses said to Joshua, Choose us out men, and go out, fight with Amalek: tomorrow I will stand on the top of the hill with the rod of God in mine hand.

(Exodus 17:10)
> So Joshua did as Moses had said to him, and fought with Amalek: and Moses, Aaron, and Hur went up to the top of the hill.

(Exodus 17:11)
> And it came to pass, when Moses held up his hand, that Israel prevailed: and when he let down his hand, Amalek prevailed.

(Exodus 17:12)
But Moses' hands were heavy; and they took a stone, and put it under him, and he sat thereon; and Aaron and Hur stayed up his hands, the one on the one side, and the other on the other side; and his hands were steady until the going down of the sun.

(Exodus 17:13)
And Joshua discomfited Amalek and his people with the edge of the sword.

(Jasher 81:54)
And they carried on a great and severe battle against Israel, and the Lord delivered Amalek and his people into the hands of Moses and the children of Israel, and into the hand of Joshua, the son of Nun, the Ephrathite, the servant of Moses.

(Jasher 81:55)
And the children of Israel smote Amalek and his people at the edge of the sword, but the battle was very sore upon the children of Israel.

(Exodus 17:14) (Jasher 81:56)
And the LORD said to Moses, Write this for a memorial in a book, and place it in the hand of Joshua, the son of Nun, your servant, and rehearse it in the ears of Joshua: and you shall command the children of Israel, saying, When you shall come to the land of Canaan, you shall utterly efface the remembrance of Amalek from under heaven, for I will utterly put out the remembrance of Amalek from under heaven.

(Jasher 81:57)
And Moses did so, and he took the book and wrote upon it these words, saying,

(Jasher 81:58)
Remember what Amalek has done to you in the road when you went forth from Egypt.

(Jasher 81:59)
Who met you in the road and smote your rear, even those that were feeble behind you when you were faint and weary.

(Jasher 81:60)
Therefore, it shall be when the Lord your God shall have given you rest from all your enemies round about in the land which the Lord your God gives you for an inheritance, to possess it, that you shall blot out the remembrance of Amalek from under heaven, you shall not forget it.

(Jasher 81:61)
And the king who shall have pity on Amalek, or upon his memory or upon his seed, behold I will require it of him, and I will cut him off from among his people.

(Jasher 81:62)
And Moses wrote all these things in a book, and he enjoined the children of Israel respecting all these matters.

(Exodus 17:15)
And Moses built an altar, and called the name of it Jehovahnissi:

(Exodus 17:16)
For he said, Because the LORD has sworn that the LORD will have war with Amalek from generation to generation.

Exodus: Chapter Eighteen

(Jasher 82:1)
And the children of Israel proceeded from Rephidim and they encamped in the wilderness of Sinai, in the third month from their going forth from Egypt.

(Exodus 18:1) (Jasher 82:2...)
When Jethro, the priest of Midian, Moses' father in law, heard of all that God had done for Moses, and for Israel his people, and that the LORD had delivered them from the hand of Egypt and had brought Israel out of Egypt;

(Exodus 18:2)
Then Jethro, Moses' father in law, took Zipporah, Moses' wife, after he had sent her back,

(Exodus 18:3)
And her two sons; of which the name of the one was Gershom; for he said, I have been an alien in a strange land:

(Exodus 18:4)
And the name of the other was Eliezer; for the God of my father, said he, was mine help, and delivered me from the sword of Pharaoh:

(Exodus 18:5) (...Jasher 82:2,3)
And at that time Reuel the Midianite / Jethro, Moses' father in law, came with his sons and Zipporah his daughter Moses'

wife to Moses into the wilderness, where he encamped at the mount of God:

(Exodus 18:6)
And he said to Moses, I your father in law Jethro am come to you, and your wife, and her two sons with her.

(Exodus 18:7) (Jasher 82:4)
And Moses went out to meet his father in law with great honor, and all Israel was with him. And Moses did obeisance, and kissed him; and they asked each other of their welfare; and they came into the tent.

(Jasher 82:5)
And Reuel and his children remained among the Israelites for many days, and Reuel knew the Lord from that day forward.

(Exodus 18:8)
And Moses told his father in law all that the LORD had done to Pharaoh and to the Egyptians for Israel's sake, and all the travail that had come upon them by the way, and how the LORD delivered them.

(Exodus 18:9)
And Jethro rejoiced for all the goodness which the LORD had done to Israel, whom he had delivered out of the hand of the Egyptians.

(Exodus 18:10)
And Jethro said, Blessed be the LORD, who has delivered you out of the hand of the Egyptians, and out of the hand of Pharaoh, who has delivered the people from under the hand of the Egyptians.

Book Six: From Goshen to Sinai

(Exodus 18:11)
Now I know that the LORD is greater than all gods: for in the thing wherein they dealt proudly he was above them.

(Exodus 18:12)
And Jethro, Moses' father in law, took a burnt offering and sacrifices for God: and Aaron came, and all the elders of Israel, to eat bread with Moses' father in law before God.

(Exodus 18:13)
And it came to pass on the morrow, that Moses sat to judge the people: and the people stood by Moses from the morning to the evening.

(Exodus 18:14)
And when Moses' father in law saw all that he did to the people, he said, What is this thing that you do to the people? Why do you sit yourself alone, and all the people stand by you from morning to even?

(Exodus 18:15)
And Moses said to his father in law, Because the people come to me to inquire of God:

(Exodus 18:16)
When they have a matter, they come to me; and I judge between one and another, and I do make them know the statutes of God, and his laws.

(Exodus 18:17)
And Moses' father in law said to him, The thing that you do is not good.

(Exodus 18:18)
> You will surely wear away, both you, and this people that is with you: for this thing is too heavy for you; you are not able to perform it yourself alone.

(Exodus 18:19)
> Hearken now to my voice, I will give you counsel, and God shall be with you: Be you for the people to God-ward, that you may bring the causes to God:

(Exodus 18:20)
> And you shall teach them ordinances and laws, and shall shew them the way wherein they must walk, and the work that they must do.

(Exodus 18:21)
> Moreover you shall provide out of all the people able men, such as fear God, men of truth, hating covetousness; and place such over them, to be rulers of thousands, and rulers of hundreds, rulers of fifties, and rulers of tens:

(Exodus 18:22)
> And let them judge the people at all seasons: and it shall be, that every great matter they shall bring to you, but every small matter they shall judge: so shall it be easier for yourself, and they shall bear the burden with you.

(Exodus 18:23)
> If you shall do this thing, and God command you so, then you shall be able to endure, and all this people shall also go to their place in peace.

(Exodus 18:24)
So Moses hearkened to the voice of his father in law, and did all that he had said.

(Exodus 18:25)
And Moses chose able men out of all Israel, and made them heads over the people, rulers of thousands, rulers of hundreds, rulers of fifties, and rulers of tens.

(Exodus 18:26)
And they judged the people at all seasons: the hard causes they brought to Moses, but every small matter they judged themselves.

(Exodus 18:27)
And Moses let his father in law depart; and he went his way into his own land.

The History of Ancient Israel

Exodus: Chapter Nineteen

(Exodus 19:1)
> In the third month, when the children of Israel were gone forth out of the land of Egypt, the same day came they into the wilderness of Sinai.

(Exodus 19:2)
> For they were departed from Rephidim, and were come to the desert of Sinai, and had pitched in the wilderness; and there Israel camped before the mount.

(Exodus 19:3)
> And Moses went up to God, and the LORD called to him out of the mountain, saying, Thus shall you say to the house of Jacob, and tell the children of Israel;

(Exodus 19:4)
> You have seen what I did to the Egyptians, and how I bare you on eagles' wings, and brought you to myself.

(Exodus 19:5)
> Now therefore, if you will obey my voice indeed, and keep my covenant, then you shall be a peculiar treasure to me above all people: for all the earth is mine:

(Exodus 19:6)
> And you shall be to me a kingdom of priests, and a holy nation. These are the words which you shall speak to the children of

Israel.

(Exodus 19:7)
And Moses came and called for the elders of the people, and laid before their faces all these words which the LORD commanded him.

(Exodus 19:8)
And all the people answered together, and said, All that the LORD has spoken we will do. And Moses returned the words of the people to the LORD.

(Exodus 19:9)
And the LORD said to Moses, Lo, I come to you in a thick cloud, that the people may hear when I speak with you, and believe you forever. And Moses told the words of the people to the LORD.

(Exodus 19:10)
And the LORD said to Moses, Go to the people, and sanctify them today and tomorrow, and let them wash their clothes,

(Exodus 19:11)
And be ready against the third day: for the third day the LORD will come down in the sight of all the people upon mount Sinai.

(Exodus 19:12)
And you shall set bounds to the people round about, saying, Take heed to yourselves, that you go not up into the mount, or touch the border of it: whosoever touches the mount shall be surely put to death:

(Exodus 19:13)
There shall not an hand touch it, but he shall surely be stoned,

or shot through; whether it be beast or man, it shall not live: when the trumpet sounds long, they shall come up to the mount.

(Exodus 19:14)
And Moses went down from the mount to the people, and sanctified the people; and they washed their clothes.

(Exodus 19:15)
And he said to the people, Be ready against the third day: come not at your wives.

(Exodus 19:16)
And it came to pass on the third day in the morning, that there were thunders and lightnings, and a thick cloud upon the mount, and the voice of the trumpet exceeding loud; so that all the people that was in the camp trembled.

(Exodus 19:17)
And Moses brought forth the people out of the camp to meet with God; and they stood at the nether part of the mount.

(Exodus 19:18)
And mount Sinai was altogether on a smoke, because the LORD descended upon it in fire: and the smoke thereof ascended as the smoke of a furnace, and the whole mount quaked greatly.

(Exodus 19:19)
And when the voice of the trumpet sounded long, and waxed louder and louder, Moses spoke, and God answered him by a voice.

(Exodus 19:20)
> And the LORD came down upon mount Sinai, on the top of the mount: and the LORD called Moses up to the top of the mount; and Moses went up.

(Exodus 19:21)
> And the LORD said to Moses, Go down, charge the people, lest they break through to the LORD to gaze, and many of them perish.

(Exodus 19:22)
> And let the priests also, which come near to the LORD, sanctify themselves, lest the LORD break forth upon them.

(Exodus 19:23)
> And Moses said to the LORD, The people cannot come up to mount Sinai: for you charged us, saying, Set bounds about the mount, and sanctify it.

(Exodus 19:24)
> And the LORD said to him, Away, get down, and you shall come up, you, and Aaron with you: but let not the priests and the people break through to come up to the LORD, lest he break forth upon them.

(Exodus 19:25)
> So Moses went down to the people, and spoke to them.

Exodus: Chapter Twenty

(Jasher 82:6)
And in the third month from the children of Israel's departure from Egypt, on the sixth day thereof, the Lord gave to Israel the ten commandments on Mount Sinai.

(Exodus 20:1)
And God spoke all these words, saying,

(Exodus 20:2)
I am the LORD your God, which have brought you out of the land of Egypt, out of the house of bondage.

(Exodus 20:3)
You shall have no other gods before me.

(Exodus 20:4)
You shall not make to you any graven image, or any likeness of anything that is in heaven above, or that is in the earth beneath, or that is in the water under the earth:

(Exodus 20:5)
You shall not bow down yourself to them, nor serve them: for I the LORD your God am a jealous God, visiting the iniquity of the fathers upon the children to the third and fourth generation of them that hate me;

(Exodus 20:6)
>And shewing mercy to thousands of them that love me, and keep my commandments.

(Exodus 20:7)
>You shall not take the name of the LORD your God in vain; for the LORD will not hold him guiltless that takes his name in vain.

(Exodus 20:8)
>Remember the sabbath day, to keep it holy.

(Exodus 20:9)
>Six days shall you labor, and do all your work:

(Exodus 20:10)
>But the seventh day is the sabbath of the LORD your God: in it you shall not do any work, you, nor your son, nor your daughter, your manservant, nor your maidservant, nor your cattle, nor your stranger that is within your gates:

(Exodus 20:11)
>For in six days the LORD made heaven and earth, the sea, and all that in them is, and rested the seventh day: why the LORD blessed the sabbath day, and hallowed it.

(Exodus 20:12)
>Honor your father and your mother: that your days may be long upon the land which the LORD your God gives you.

(Exodus 20:13)
>You shall not kill.

(Exodus 20:14)
You shall not commit adultery.

(Exodus 20:15)
You shall not steal.

(Exodus 20:16)
You shall not bear false witness against your neighbor.

(Exodus 20:17)
You shall not covet your neighbor's house, you shall not covet your neighbor's wife, nor his manservant, nor his maidservant, nor his ox, nor his donkey, nor any thing that is your neighbor's.

(Jasher 82:7)
And all Israel heard all these commandments, and all Israel rejoiced exceedingly in the Lord on that day.

(Exodus 20:18)
And all the people saw the thunderings, and the lightnings, and the noise of the trumpet, and the mountain smoking: and when the people saw it, they removed, and stood afar off.

(Exodus 20:19)
And they said to Moses, You speak with us, and we will hear: but let not God speak with us, lest we die.

(Exodus 20:20)
And Moses said to the people, Fear not: for God is come to prove you, and that his fear may be before your faces, that you sin not.

(Exodus 20:21)
> And the people stood afar off, and Moses drew near to the thick darkness where God was.

(Exodus 20:22)
> And the LORD said to Moses, Thus you shall say to the children of Israel, You have seen that I have talked with you from heaven.

(Exodus 20:23)
> You shall not make with me gods of silver, neither shall you make to you gods of gold.

(Exodus 20:24)
> An altar of earth you shall make to me, and shall sacrifice thereon your burnt offerings, and your peace offerings, your sheep, and your oxen: in all places where I record my name I will come to you, and I will bless you.

(Exodus 20:25)
> And if you will make me an altar of stone, you shall not build it of hewn stone: for if you lift up your tool upon it, you have polluted it.

(Exodus 20:26)
> Neither shall you go up by steps to mine altar, that your nakedness be not discovered thereon.

Final Notes

We hope your journey is enriched and you are blessed through the production of THE HISTORY OF ANCIENT ISRAEL.

Please take a moment to submit a kind review online and let others know about this book series.

Check out the rest of the books in this series:

The History of Ancient Israel
Completely Synchronizing the Extra-Biblical Apocrypha Books of Enoch, Jasher, and Jubilees

Book 1:   From Adam to Noah
Book 2:   From Noah to Abraham
Book 3:   From Abraham to Israel
Book 4:   From Israel to Egypt
Book 5:   From Egypt to Goshen
Book 6:   From Goshen to Sinai
Book 7:   From Sinai to the Tabernacle
Book 8:   Through the Book of Leviticus
Book 9:   Through the Book of Numbers
Book 10: Through the Book of Joshua

www.ingramcontent.com/pod-product-compliance
Lightning Source LLC
Chambersburg PA
CBHW022007120526
44592CB00034B/536